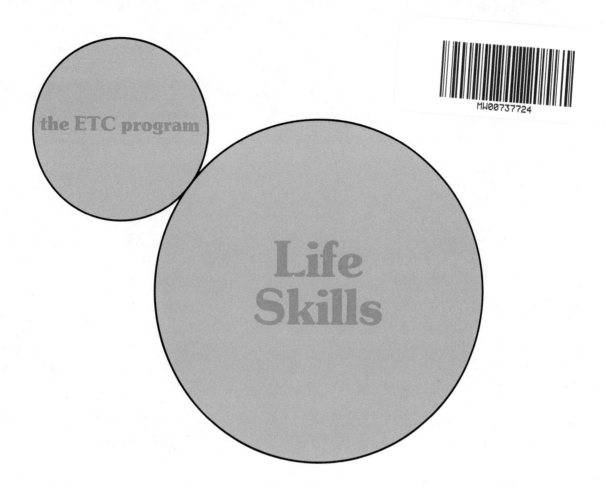

the ETC program

Life Skills

Skills Book

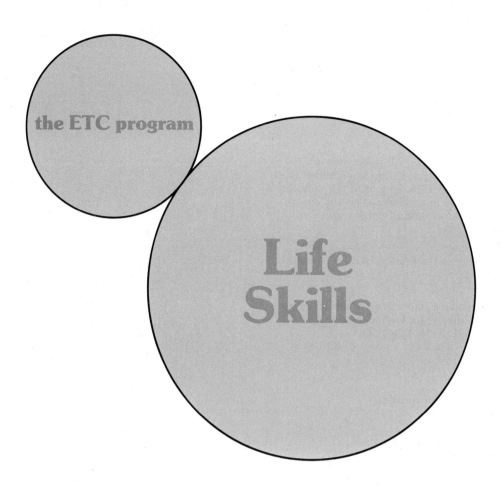

the ETC program

Life Skills

Skills Book

Elaine Kirn
West Los Angeles College

McGraw-Hill, Inc.
New York St. Louis San Francisco Auckland Bogotá
Caracas Lisbon London Madrid Mexico City Milan
Montreal New Delhi San Juan Singapore
Sydney Tokyo Toronto

First Edition

4 5 6 7 8 9 BBC BBC 9 9 8 7 6 5

Library of Congress Cataloging-in-Publication Data

Kirn, Elaine.
    The *ETC* programLife skills: a competency-based skills book
    1. English language—Textbooks for foreign speakers.
2. Life Skill.   I. Title.   II. Title: Life Skills.
PE1128.K483   1988   428.2'4   87-35756
ISBN 0-07-553745-1

Manufactured in the United States of America

Series design and production: Etcetera Graphics
                    Canoga Park, California
Cover design: Juan Vargas, Vargas/Williams Design
Illustrations: Etcetera Graphics
Artist: Terry Wilson
Photo Research: Marian Hartsough
Photos: Sally Gati
Typesetting: Etcetera Graphics

Contents

Preface   **ix**

Introduction   Names and Letters   1

Competencies: Using the letters of the alphabet • Meeting people • Using greetings and expressions for departures • Recognizing first and last names • Spelling names aloud • Printing and signing names

CHAPTER 1   Things   6

Competencies: Naming and describing things • Using numbers 1-12 • Understanding conversations about things • Making and answering requests for things • Expressing lack of understanding • Using polite expressions • Reading lists of things, times on a clock, and signs

PART ONE   Vocabulary   8
PART TWO   Listening   10
PART THREE   Grammar in Conversation   12
PART FOUR   Reading and Writing   14

CHAPTER 2   Information   16

Competencies: Understanding instructions • Using numbers 13-90 • Understanding names, addresses, and telephone numbers • Asking for, giving, and writing personal information • Reading signs

PART ONE   Vocabulary   18
PART TWO   Listening   22
PART THREE   Grammar in Conversation   24
PART FOUR   Reading and Writing   27

CHAPTER 3   Help   31

Competencies: Making and answering requests for help • Using numbers 20-200 • Expressing personal information (height, weight, year of birth, etc.) • Comparing units of measurement • Asking and giving directions • Reading signs

PART ONE   Vocabulary   33
PART TWO   Listening   36
PART THREE   Grammar in Conversation   38
PART FOUR   Reading and Writing   42

CHAPTER 4   Food and Money   45

Competencies: Doing simple math (addition and multiplication) • Expressing needs and wants • Ordering food • Asking for and giving change • Understanding price lists • Reading signs

PART ONE   Vocabulary   47
PART TWO   Listening   51
PART THREE   Grammar in Conversation   53
PART FOUR   Reading and Writing   56

CHAPTER 5   Times and Places   59

Competencies: Reading and telling the time, day, and date • Describing the weather • Expressing location • Making social appointments • Reading calendars • Reading thermometers and weather maps • Understanding time zones

PART ONE   Vocabulary   61
PART TWO   Listening   65
PART THREE   Grammar in Conversation   67
PART FOUR   Reading and Writing   71

CHAPTER 6   The Body   75

Competencies: Telling clothing sizes and prices • Describing physical feelings, illnesses, and health habits • Understanding and filling out medical forms • Reading medicine labels

PART ONE   Vocabulary   77
PART TWO   Listening   79
PART THREE   Grammar in Conversation   81
PART FOUR   Reading and Writing   86

CHAPTER 7   People   89

Competencies: Locating countries on a world map • Recognizing family relationships • Recognizing job titles and work descriptions • Using the post office • Giving and taking telephone messages • Asking and telling about relatives and friends • Addressing envelopes • Understanding postal and telephone information

PART ONE   Vocabulary   91
PART TWO   Listening   94
PART THREE   Grammar in Conversation   96
PART FOUR   Reading and Writing   100

CHAPTER **8** Emergencies 104

Competencies: Recognizing emergency situations ● Calling emergency numbers ● Knowing steps in simple first aid ● Reading warning signs

PART ONE Vocabulary **106**
PART TWO Listening **108**
PART THREE Grammar in Conversation **110**
PART FOUR Reading and Writing **114**

CHAPTER **9** Work 118

Competencies: Knowing how to look for work ● Describing past work, job skills, and education ● Understanding educational requirements ● Understanding "help wanted" ads ● Reading and filling out applications for employment

PART ONE Vocabulary **120**
PART TWO Listening **122**
PART THREE Grammar in Conversation **124**
PART FOUR Reading and Writing **130**

CHAPTER **10** Fun 132

Competencies: Asking and telling about interests and plans ● Knowing about recreational activities ● Understanding party invitations ● Understanding T.V. and radio schedules ● Reading recreation programs and information

PART ONE Vocabulary **134**
PART TWO Listening **135**
PART THREE Grammar in Conversation **137**
PART FOUR Reading and Writing **141**

Preface

Language is me.
Language is you.
Language is people.
Language is what people do.
Language is loving and hurting.
Language is clothes, faces, gestures, responses.
Language is imagining, designing, creating, destroying.
Language is control and persuasion.
Language is communication.
Language is laughter.
Language is growth.
Language is me.
The limits of my language are the limits of my world.

And you can't package *that* up in a book, can you?

—*New Zealand Curriculum Development*

No, you can't package language in a book or even a whole program of books, but you have to start somewhere.

About the *ETC* Program

ETC is a six-level ESL (English as a second language) program for adults who are learning English to improve their lives and work skills. The material of this level is divided into two books, carefully coordinated, chapter by chapter, in theme, competency goals, grammar, and vocabulary. For a visual representation of the scope and sequence of the program, see the back cover of any volume.

ETC has been designed for maximum efficiency and flexibility. To choose the materials most suitable for your particular teaching situation, decide on the appropriate level by assessing the ability and needs of the students you expect to be teaching. The competency descriptions included in each instructor's manual ("About This Level") will aid you in your assessment.

About This Book

The core of *ETC Life Skills* is this skills book. It is four skills: listening, speaking, reading, and writing. All listening sections, marked with a cassette symbol, are available on audiocassette.

Organization

Like most other books in the program, the *ETC Life Skills: Skills Book* consists of an introduction and ten chapters, each divided into four parts with specific purposes.

● *Part One: Vocabulary* presents the key vocabulary of the chapter, with visual illustrations of the meanings.

• *Part Two: Listening* provides comprehension activities to help students develop listening skills: identifying situations, understanding content words, and performing practical tasks in response to aural cues.

• *Part Three: Grammar in Conversation* provides speaking practice in simulated practical situations.

• *Part Four: Reading and Writing* presents greatly simplified versions of the kinds of reading material students are likely to encounter in everyday life, followed by practice in practical writing tasks.

Symbols

The following symbols appear throughout the text:

     activity on cassette tape

 ✻ a challenging activity designed for more advanced students

Available Ancillaries

A complete set of audiotapes accompanies this book. The instructors's annotated edition for this text includes:

• a general introduction to the *ETC* program, this level, and this book

• general suggestions for teaching techniques to use in presenting the various kinds of activities

• page-by-page teacher's notes next to the reduced pages of the student text to which they refer

• an answer key provided on the reduced pages

• a pronunciation supplement of worksheets that can be duplicated and handed out to students

• a vocabulary list, chapter by chapter

• a tapescript for all material recorded on cassette

Acknowledgments

To Etcetera, ETC, ETC, because we finally did it.

Appreciation beyond frustration goes to the many class testers and reviewers, reviewers, reviewers—whose opinions lie at the core of the *ETC* program. Thanks to the following reviewers, whose comments both favorable and critical, were of great value in the development of *ETC Life Skills*:

Fred Allen, Elsa Auerbach, Joseph Berkowitz, John Boyd, Mary Ann Boyd, Jeffrey P. Bright, Lori B. Brooks, Christine Bunn, Elizabeth Chafcouloff, Mary Ann Christison, Dorothy Clemens, Patricia Costello, John P. Dermody, Nina Glandini, Sandra Hagman, Anne Lindell Hagiwara, Mary M. Hurst, Dona Kelley, Lynne R. Madden, Janet McColl, Kathy Michas, Barbara Moten, Alice Perlman, Denise Quinn, Judith Rodby, Edward Schiffer, Kent Sutherland, Judith Tanka, Anne Topple, Betsey Warrick, Ann Wederspahn, and Anita L. Wenden.

The author wishes to thank the staff at McGraw-Hill, Inc.:
- Eirik Borve and Karen Judd—for keeping promises,
- Lesley Walsh—for being as efficient as ever,
- Marian Hartsough—for communicating where need be, and
- Edith Brady, Cynthia Ward, and the sales staff—for what is yet to come.

Heartfelt thanks to the staff and supporters of Etcetera Graphics, Canoga Park, California:
- Terry Wilson—for his inspired artwork and patience,
- Cindra Tardif—for expert typesetting, and
- Sheila Clark—for alert and patient production,

and gratitude, appreciation, and love to
- Anthony Thorne-Booth—for his management, expertise, and hard work,
- Karol Roff—for helping, helping, helping,
- Sally Kostal—for jumping in to rescue us and to keep us calm,
- Chuck Alessio—for everything and more

and to Andi Kirn—for putting up with it all.

E.K.

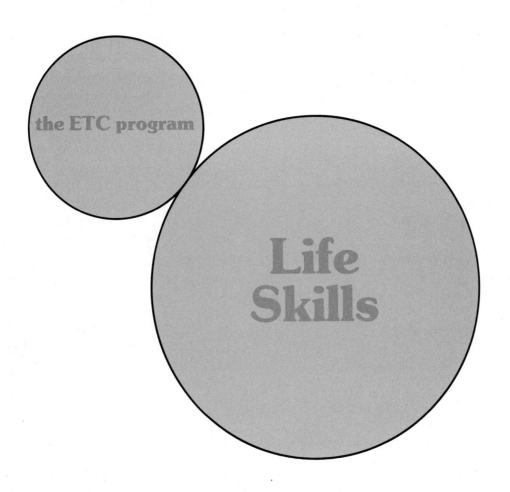

the ETC program

Life
Skills

Skills Book

Names
and
Letters

Introduction

COMPETENCIES:
Using the letters of the alphabet
Meeting people
Using greetings and expressions for departures
Recognizing first and last names
Spelling names aloud
Printing and signing names

1

Names

First Name	Last Name	First Name	Last Name
Ron	Smith	Su-Yan	Wong
Ann	Taft-Hunt	Rosa	Gonzalez

last name = family name

A. Have conversations.

The Letters of the Alphabet

A B C D E F G H I J K L M N O P Q R S T U V W X Y Z

B. Look and write the letters.

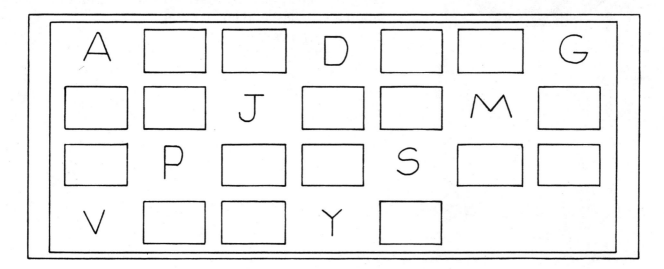

Printed Letters

CAPITAL
A B C D E F G H I J K L M
N O P Q R S T U V W X Y Z

small
a b c d e f g h i j k l m
n o p q r s t u v w x y z

Names

First Name	Last Name		Last Name	,	First Name
Ann	Smith		Smith	,	Ann
Ron	Taft-Hunt		Taft-Hunt	,	Ron
Li-Li	Lin		Lin	,	Li-Li

_____ **C. Print your name.**

_____   _____ , _____
    FIRST   LAST   LAST ,   FIRST

Handwriting

CAPITAL
A B C D E F G H I J K L M
N O P Q R S T U V W X Y Z

small
a b c d e f g h i j k l m
n o p q r s t u v w x y z

_____ **D. Use handwriting for your name.**

_____
        SIGNATURE

E. Use printing and handwriting for your names.

1. _____ , _____   _____
     LAST ,   FIRST   SIGNATURE

2. _____ , _____   _____
     LAST ,   FIRST   SIGNATURE

3. _____ , _____   _____
     LAST ,   FIRST   SIGNATURE

4. _____ , _____   _____
     LAST ,   FIRST   SIGNATURE

5. _____ , _____   _____
     LAST ,   FIRST   SIGNATURE

6. _____ , _____   _____
     LAST ,   FIRST   SIGNATURE

7. _____ , _____   _____
     LAST ,   FIRST   SIGNATURE

8. _____ , _____   _____
     LAST ,   FIRST   SIGNATURE

*F. Have conversations and write names.

_____ *G. Have conversations.

CHAPTER

1

Things

COMPETENCIES:

Naming and describing things
Using numbers 1-12
Understanding conversations about things
Making and answering requests for things
Expressing lack of understanding
Using polite expressions
Reading lists of things, times on a clock, and signs

GRAMMAR FOCUS:

Singular and plural nouns
Adjectives before nouns
Prepositions

A notebook, please.

PART ONE / VOCABULARY

● Things ● Numbers 1-12

 A. Look and write the letters *A–I*.

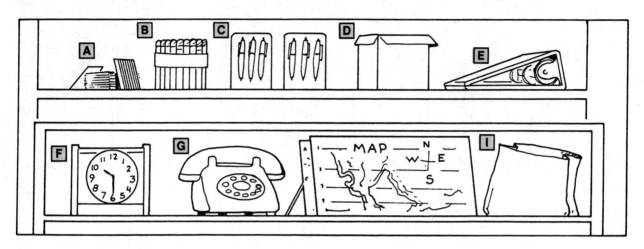

1. _F_ a clock   4. ___ a box   7. ___ pens

2. ___ a telephone   5. ___ a bag   8. ___ maps

3. ___ a notebook   6. ___ pencils   9. ___ cards

B. Circle the words.

1.
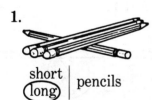

short
(long) | pencils

2.

a | black
white | pen

3.
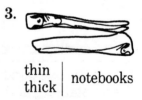

thin
thick | notebooks

4.
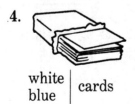

white
blue | cards

5.

long
short | books

6.
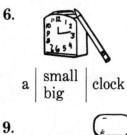

a | small
big | clock

7.
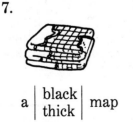

a | black
thick | map

8.
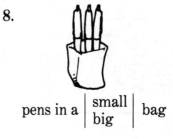

pens in a | small
big | bag

9.

a | thin
big | box of books

Numbers (How Many?)

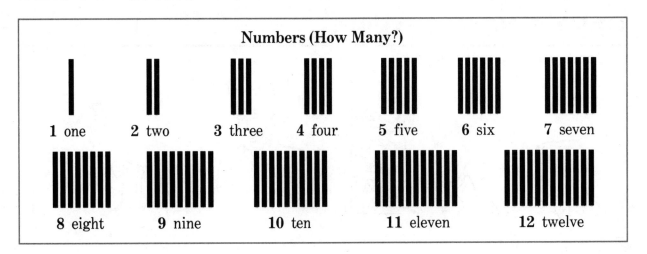

1 one   2 two   3 three   4 four   5 five   6 six   7 seven

8 eight   9 nine   10 ten   11 eleven   12 twelve

C. Look and write the numbers.

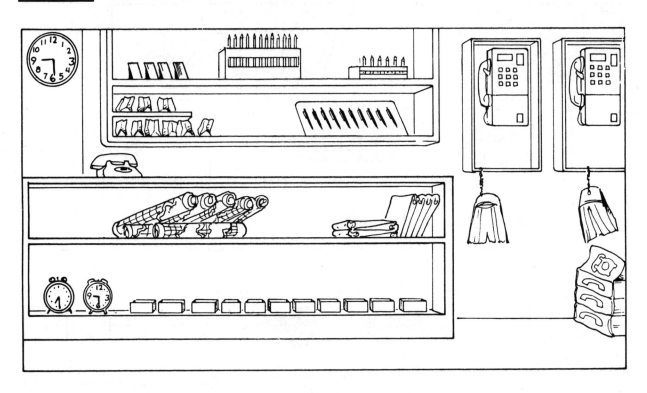

1. _7_ maps

2. ___ boxes

3. ___ bags

4. ___ telephones

5. ___ telephone books

6. ___ white cards

7. ___ black pens

8. ___ thin notebooks

9. ___ big clock

10. ___ small clocks

11. ___ short pencils

12. ___ long pencils in a box

PART TWO / LISTENING

● Conversations about Things

A. Listen and write the numbers 1–4.

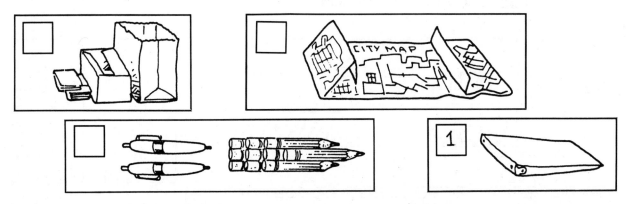

B. Listen and write the numbers.

1	2	3	5	8	12

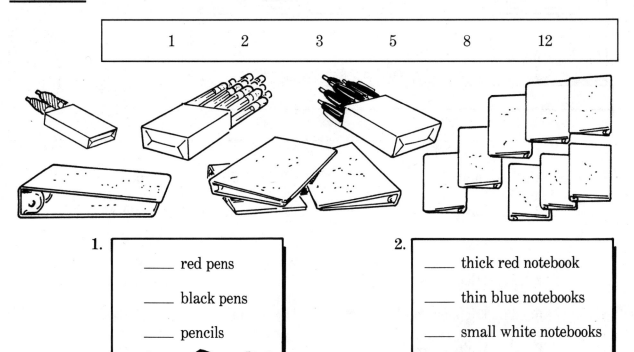

1.
____ red pens

____ black pens

____ pencils

2.
____ thick red notebook

____ thin blue notebooks

____ small white notebooks

C. **Listen and circle the words.**

PART THREE / GRAMMAR IN CONVERSATION

● Singular and Plural Nouns ● Adjectives before Nouns ● Prepositions
● Requests for Things ● Lack of Understanding ● Polite Expressions

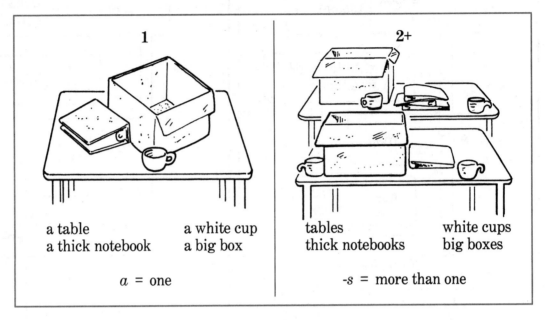

1	2+
a table a white cup	tables white cups
a thick notebook a big box	thick notebooks big boxes
a = one	*-s* = more than one

 A.   **Listen and talk.**

1. a: **Six pencils**, please.   Nine pens

    b: How many?

    a: **Six**. No, sorry.   Nine.

       Eight pencils.   Twelve pens.

    b: **All right**.   Sure.

2. a: Two **maps**.   notebooks

    b: **O.K. Big**? **Small**?   Oh. White? Blue?

    a: Two **small maps**.   blue notebooks

3. b: A **bag**?   box

    a: **Excuse me**?   Sorry, what?

    b: A big **bag**?   box

    a: Oh. **Yes, please**.   All right.

       Thank you.   Thanks.

*B. Have conversations.

1. 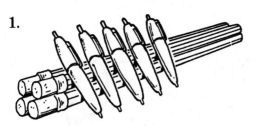   2.    3.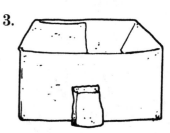

EXAMPLE: **a:** Four long pencils, please.
b: How many?
a: Four. And five pens.

a box	of	notebooks	a telephone	on	the table
a cup	for	long pencils	cards	in	a small box

 C. Listen and talk.

a: A box of **pencils**, please.   pens

b: Sure. And **class cards**, too?   notebooks

a: **Yes, please.**   Right.

b: **On the table.**   In the bag.

PART FOUR / READING AND WRITING

● Times on a Clock   ● Signs

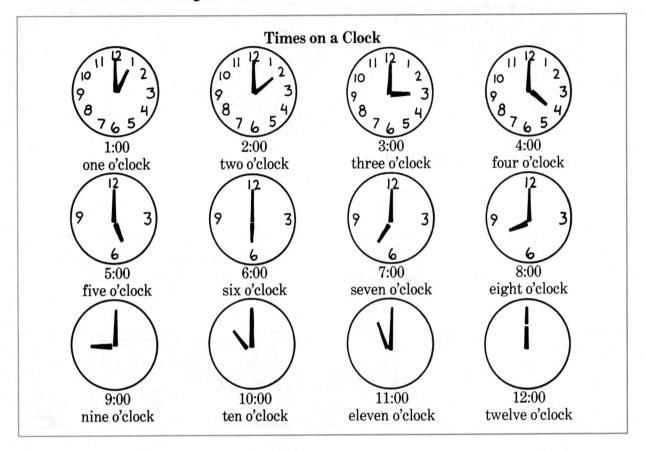

Times on a Clock

1:00 one o'clock	2:00 two o'clock	3:00 three o'clock	4:00 four o'clock
5:00 five o'clock	6:00 six o'clock	7:00 seven o'clock	8:00 eight o'clock
9:00 nine o'clock	10:00 ten o'clock	11:00 eleven o'clock	12:00 twelve o'clock

___ A.   **Write the numbers *1–12*.**

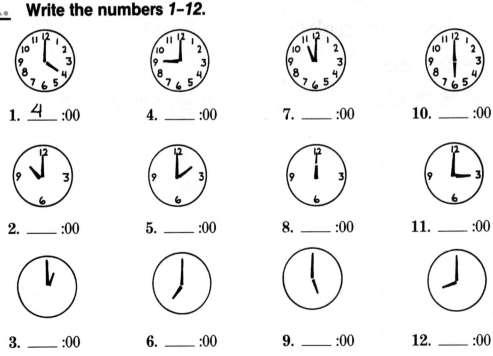

1. _4_ :00   4. ___ :00   7. ___ :00   10. ___ :00

2. ___ :00   5. ___ :00   8. ___ :00   11. ___ :00

3. ___ :00   6. ___ :00   9. ___ :00   12. ___ :00

B. Look and write the letters *A–G*.

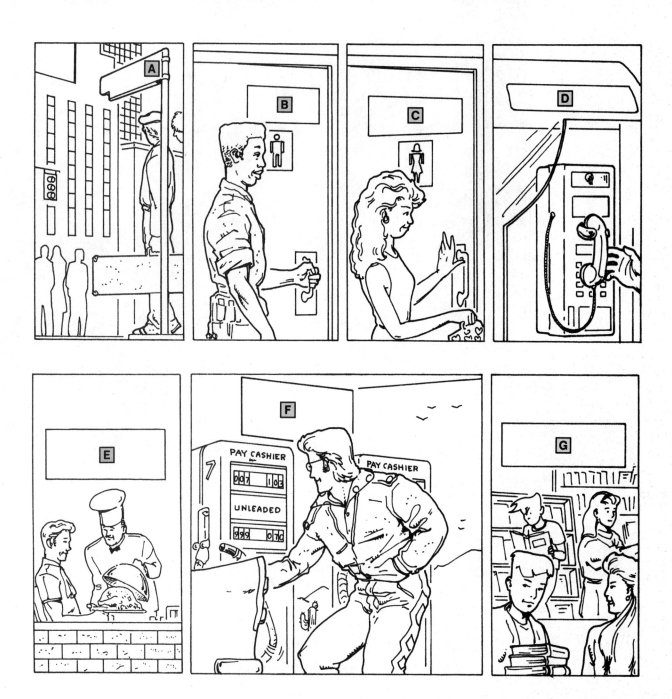

1. B̲ MEN'S RESTROOM

2. ___ WOMEN'S RESTROOM

3. ___ TELEPHONE

4. ___ GAS

5. ___ FOOD

6. ___ MAIN STREET

7. ___ BOOKSTORE

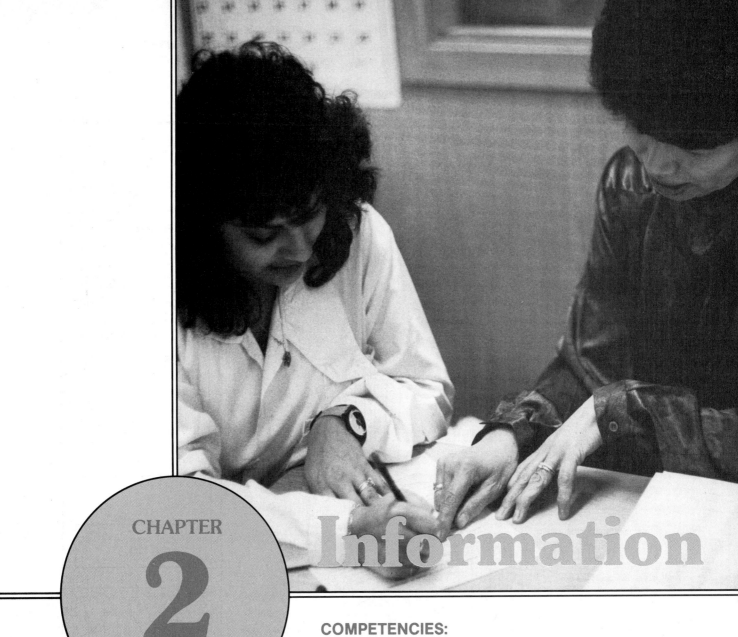

CHAPTER

2

Information

COMPETENCIES:
Understanding instructions
Using numbers 13-90
Understanding names, addresses, and
 telephone numbers
Asking for, giving, and writing personal information
Reading signs

GRAMMAR FOCUS:
Imperative verbs
Possessive adjectives

Please tell me your name and address.

PART ONE / VOCABULARY

● Instructions ● Kinds of information ● Numbers 13-90

A. Look and write the letters *A–I*.

A.

B.

C.
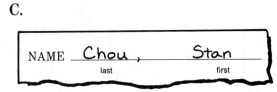

1. __C__ Put your last name first.

2. _____ Please take a card.

3. _____ Don't write in pen. Use a pencil.

D.
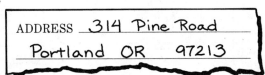

E.

38315

F.

4. _____ Sign your name on the line, please.

5. _____ Don't forget the zip code.

6. _____ Now print the information on the card.

G.

H.

I.

7. _____ Give me your card, please.

8. _____ Now look at the map.

9. _____ Don't bring me your notebook.

B. Look and write the letters *A–F*.

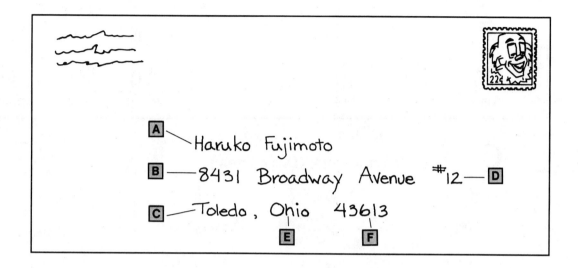

1. <u>A</u> her first name

2. ___ the apartment number

3. ___ the street number

4. ___ the state

5. ___ the zip code

6. ___ the city

Write the letters *G–L*.

7. ___ his last name

8. ___ his signature

9. ___ the street name

10. ___ his telephone number

11. ___ the area code

12. ___ his class

Numbers

12	13	14	15	16	17	18	19
twelve	thirteen	fourteen	fifteen	sixteen	seventeen	eighteen	nineteen
20	**30**	**40**	**50**	**60**	**70**	**80**	**90**
twenty	thirty	forty	fifty	sixty	seventy	eighty	ninety

C. Match the numbers. (Draw lines.)

1. 16   seventy   6. 90   eighty

2. 60   fifty   7. 15   fifteen

3. 70   seventeen   8. 19   nineteen

4. 17   sixteen   9. 18   ninety

5. 50   sixty   10. 80   eighteen

D. Write and read the numbers.

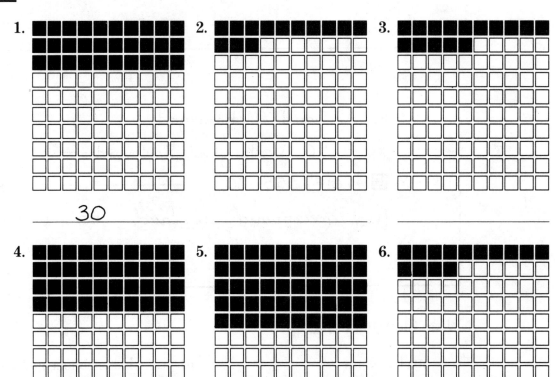

1. _____30_____

2. _____

3. _____

4. _____

5. _____

6. _____

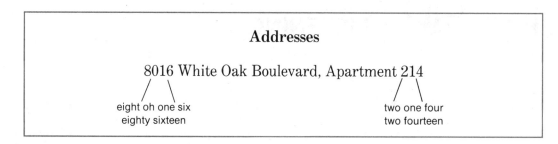

Addresses

8016 White Oak Boulevard, Apartment 214

eight oh one six   two one four
eighty sixteen   two fourteen

E. Circle the words for numbers.

1.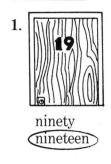
ninety
(nineteen)

2.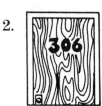
thirty six
three oh six

3.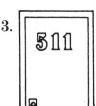
five eleven
fifty one one

4.
thirteen oh
one thirty

5.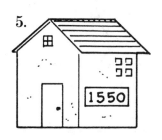
fifteen fifty
fifty fifteen

6.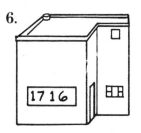
seventy sixty
seventeen sixteen

7.
twenty eighteen
two oh eighty

8.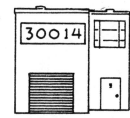
three oh oh one four
thirteen oh forty

F. Write the numbers.

1. Apartment ___30___ (thirty)

2. Room _____ (one oh seven)

3. Apartment _____ (two eleven)

4. Room _____ (six fourteen)

5. _____ Elm Street (five oh eight one three)

6. _____ Grand Boulevard (twenty twenty)

7. _____ Central Avenue (fifteen ninety)

8. _____ Brown Road (twelve seventeen)

PART TWO / LISTENING

● Names, Addresses, and Telephone Numbers

 A.   **Listen and write the numbers 1–4.**

B.   **Listen and write the numbers.**

18	30	216	305	4015	33132

1.

CLASS CARD   ENGLISH 2

Name   <u>Park</u>   <u>Sung Hee</u>
       last   first

Address   [ ]   <u>Oak Ave.</u>   [ ]
      number   street   apt.

<u>Miami</u>   <u>Florida</u>   [ ]
city   state   zip

2.

ADDRESS BOOK

Name   <u>Cruz, Martin</u>

Address   [ ]   <u>Green St.</u>   [ ]

Phone ([ ])   <u>555-0981</u>

 C.   **Listen and write the words.**

Missouri	Colorado	Illinois	Texas	Road	Kline

1.

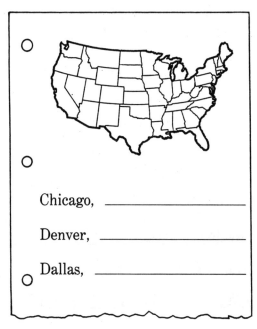

Chicago, _____

Denver, _____

Dallas, _____

2.

<u>Maria</u>

<u>1114 Spring</u>

<u>Kansas City</u>

64118

PART THREE / GRAMMAR IN CONVERSATION

● Imperative Verbs ● Possessive Adjectives ● Personal Information

Use	a pen.		Sign	your name.
Don't use	a pencil.		Don't print	your name.

 A. **Listen and talk.**

1. **a:** Take a class card, please.
   __Write__ the information.   Print
   b: Excuse me. Pencil __O.K.__?   all right
   a: No. Please __use a pen__.   don't use a pencil

2. **a:** Put your last name __first__.   last
   Don't forget the __zip code__.   area code
   b: __And then__?   Now what?
   a: Don't __give__ me the card   bring
   Put it __here__.   in the box

B. **Make sentences.**

EXAMPLES: 1. Take a card.
            Take a pencil, too.
            Don't use a pen.

1.

3.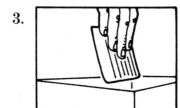

2.
   Name Smith, Ann
   Address 161 Oak St.
   Dallas, Texas   79968

my card   **your** card   **our** cards   **your** cards

his card   **her** card   **their** cards

**C.** **Listen and talk.**

1. **a:** Please tell me **your** name.   his
   b: **My** family name? Wong.   His
   a: And **your** first name?   his
   b: **My Ling**.   Danny.
   a: Spell it, please.
   b: **M-y L-i-n-g**.   D-a-n-n-y.

2. **a:** **Our** address is   Their
      1318 Oak **Street**.   Avenue
   b: Give me the **city**, too.   state
   a: **Detroit**.   Michigan.
   b: **Thank you**.   Thanks.

3. **a:** What's **our** phone number?   your
   b: **555-7629**.   555-1107.
   a: Don't forget the area code.
   b: **212**.   619.

D. Have conversations.

EXAMPLE: 1. **a:** What's her name?
  b: Rose Salib.
  a: Tell me her address, please.
  b: 1350 First Avenue.
  a: Give me the city, too.

1. her

STUDENT CARD

Salib, Rose
1350 First Avenue
Chicago, Illinois 60613
(312) 555-1213

2. his

STUDENT CARD

Lin, Yan-Ping
7091 Frisco Road
Dallas, Texas 79968
(214) 555-8004

3. their

STUDENT CARD

Ito, Hisao
1990 Jack Street
Apartment 111
Wells, Kansas 67488
(913) 555-8885

STUDENT CARD

Ito, Haruko
1990 Jack Street
Apartment 111
Wells, Kansas 67488
(913) 555-8885

***4.** your

STUDENT CARD

NAME _____
              last   first

ADDRESS _____
                number   street

_____
city   state   zip

PHONE _____
          area code   number

PART FOUR / READING AND WRITING

● Personal Information ● Signs

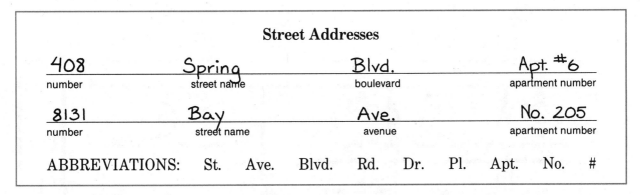

Street Addresses

408	Spring	Blvd.	Apt. #6
number	street name	boulevard	apartment number

8131	Bay	Ave.	No. 205
number	street name	avenue	apartment number

ABBREVIATIONS: St.   Ave.   Blvd.   Rd.   Dr.   Pl.   Apt.   No.   #

A. Print the abbreviations.

1. 921 East York   Apt.   9
   Boulevard   Apartment

2. 1107 Green   501
   Avenue   Number

3. 122 School   5
   Place   Number

4. 830 Hume
   Road

5. 8 Stone
   Drive

6. 4013 Pine
   Street

B. Print your street address here.

_____   _____   _____
number   street name   apartment number

Cities and States / Provinces

Detroit	MI	48226	Los Angeles	CA	90016
city	state	zip code	city	state	zip code

ABBREVIATIONS: CA   NY   TX   FL   MA   MI   PA   BC

C. Print the abbreviations for state or province names.

1. San Francisco   CA
   California

2. Miami
   Florida

3. Detroit
   Michigan

4. Vancouver
   British Columbia

D. Print your address here.

_____

city   state   zip code

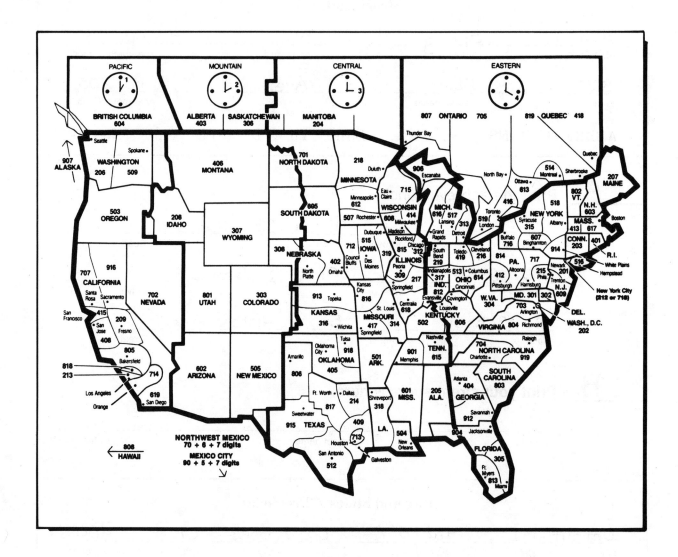

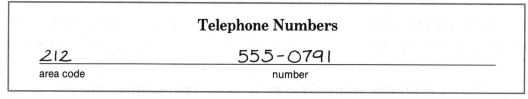

Telephone Numbers

_212_   _555-0791_
_____
area code   number

E. Put your telephone number here.

_____

area code   number

F.　Print the information about you.

NAME _____ , _____
　　　　　　　last　　　　　　　　　　　　first

ADDRESS _____
　　　　　number　　　　　street　　　　　apartment

_____ , _____
　　　　city　　　　　　　state　　　　　zip code

TELEPHONE _____ _____
　　　　　area code　　　　　　　　number

*G.　Talk and print the information.

1.

NAME _____
　　　　　last　　　　　　　　　　first

ADDRESS _____
　　　　　number　　　　　street　　　　　apartment

TELEPHONE _____
　　　　　area code　　　　　　　number

2.

NAME _____
　　　　　last　　　　　　　　　　first

ADDRESS _____
　　　　　number　　　　　street　　　　　apartment

TELEPHONE _____
　　　　　area code　　　　　　　number

3.

NAME _____
　　　　　last　　　　　　　　　　first

ADDRESS _____
　　　　　number　　　　　street　　　　　apartment

TELEPHONE _____
　　　　　area code　　　　　　　number

H. Look and write the letters A–G.

1. C WALK

2. ___ DON'T WALK

3. ___ DO NOT ENTER

4. ___ NO SMOKING

5. ___ TAKE ONE

6. ___ EAT HERE

7. ___ STOP

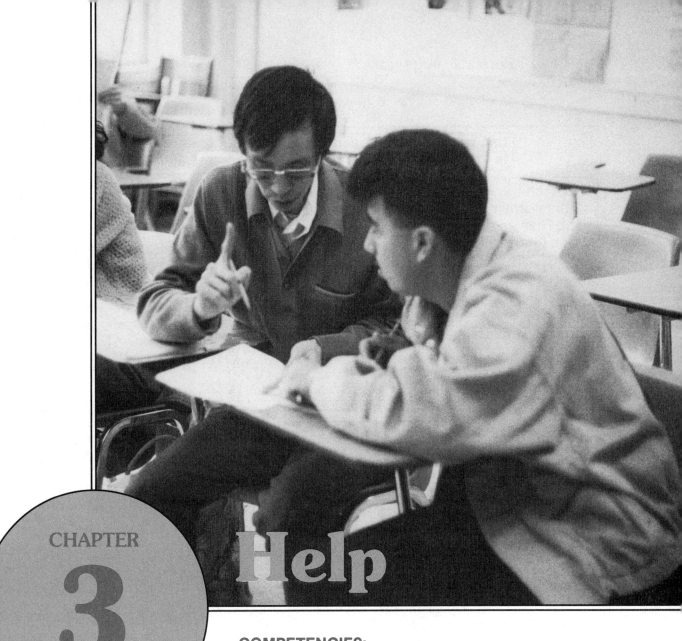

Help

COMPETENCIES:
Making and answering requests for help
Using numbers 20-200
Expressing language ability
Asking and telling the time
Expressing personal information (height, weight,
   year of birth, etc.)
Comparing units of measurement
Asking and giving directions
Reading signs

GRAMMAR FOCUS:
Can/can't
Adverbs and prepositional phrases

Can you help me, please?

PART ONE / VOCABULARY

- Requests for Help ● Numbers 20-200 ● Personal Information ● Clock Times
- Directions

 Look and write the letters A-H.

1. __G__ Can you tell me the time, please?

__H__ It's about 9:50.

2. _____ Can you please give me directions?

_____ Walk south one block on Oak Avenue and turn left. Go straight on Main Street.

3. _____ Can I take an English class?

_____ Tell me about your skills.

4. _____ Can I get a student I.D.?

_____ Give me your height, weight, and year of birth.

Numbers 20-200

20 twenty	21 twenty-one	22 twenty-two	23 twenty-three	24 twenty-four
25 twenty-five	26 twenty-six	27 twenty-seven	28 twenty-eight	29 twenty-nine
105 one hundred five	131 one hundred thirty-one	142 one hundred forty-two	199 one hundred ninety-nine	200 two hundred

Time on a Clock

three oh eight   six fifteen   one thirty-five   eight fifty

B. Match and read the times.

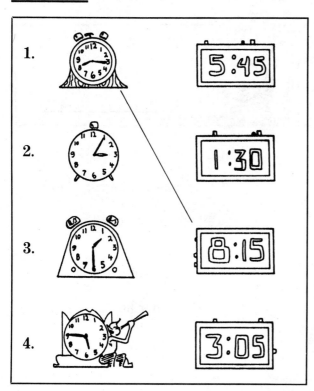

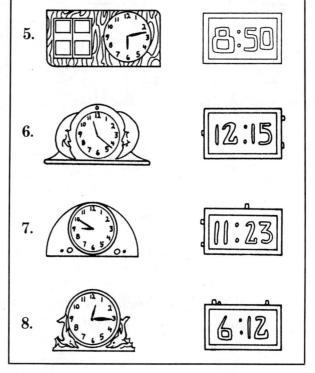

Personal Information

5'4"
5-04

five (feet) four (inches)
five foot four

162 lbs.

one hundred sixty-two pounds
one sixty-two

1958

nineteen fifty-eight

C. Read and write the numbers.

1. five feet nine inches = ____5____ ' ____9____ "

2. one hundred twenty-two pounds = ____122____ lbs.

3. the year nineteen forty-eight = _____

4. one hundred seventy pounds = _____

5. the year nineteen sixty-nine = _____

6. five feet three inches = _____ - _____

7. six foot one = _____ ' _____ "

8. nineteen fifty = _____

9. one sixty-eight = _____

10. four eleven = _____ - _____

D. Look and write the letters.

1. __A__ her name

2. ____ her address

3. ____ female

4. ____ her height

5. ____ her weight in pounds

6. ____ her hair color

7. ____ her eye color

8. ____ her year of birth

DRIVER LICENSE

Jane McBride Watanabe **A**
13206 Central Ave., Apt. 6 } **B**
San Francisco CA 94103

sex	hair	eyes	ht	wt	yr/birth
F	brown	blue	5-02	119	1930
C	**D**	**E**	**F**	**G**	**H**

PART TWO / LISTENING

● Requests for Help

 A. **Listen and write the numbers 1–4.**

B. **Listen and follow the instructions.**

1. Write X's in the boxes. Write a number on the line.

ENGLISH SKILLS

	yes	no
UNDERSTAND	☐	☒
SPEAK	☐	☐
READ	☐	☐
WRITE	☐	☐

CLASS LEVEL _____

2. Draw the time on the clock.

3. Write the numbers and words.

2   6   185   1970   br   bl

WESTEND SCHOOL
STUDENT CARD

Peter   Miller
name

M ☐ ' ☐ " ☐ lbs.
sex   height   weight

☐
hair color

☐
eye color

☐
year of birth

4. Draw a line for the directions.

BUS

BOOKSTORE   GAS

OAK AVE.

PHONE

SCHOOL

ELM ST.   START
HERE

PART THREE / GRAMMAR IN CONVERSATION

- *Can/Can't*   Adverbs and Prepositional Phrases ● Language Ability   Time
- Personal Information ● Directions

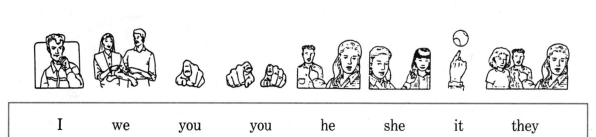

| I | we | you | you | he | she | it | they |

Can | I / we | take a class here?   Yes, / No, | you | can. / can't.

Can | you / your | brother / sister / friends | speak English?

Yes, / No, | I / we / he / she / they | can. / can't.

I / We | can / can't | take Level 3.

A.   Listen and talk.

a: Can **you and your friend understand** English well?   your mother / read

b: Yes, **we** can.   she

a: Can **you speak** it well?   she write

b: No, **we** can't.   she

　 Can **we** take a class here?   she

a: Yes, **you** can.   she

　 You can have Level Two.   She

B. Have conversations.

EXAMPLE: 1. a: Can Hisao understand English?
          b: Yes, he can.
          a: Can he speak English?
          b: No, he can't.

1. he

ENGLISH SKILLS

NAME Ito, Hisao

	yes	no
UNDERSTAND	☒	☐
SPEAK	☐	☒
READ	☐	☒
WRITE	☐	☒

CLASS LEVEL 1

2. she

ENGLISH SKILLS

NAME Salib, Rose.

	yes	no
UNDERSTAND	☐	✓
SPEAK	☐	✓
READ	✓	☐
WRITE	✓	☐

CLASS LEVEL 2

3. they

ENGLISH SKILLS

NAME Cruz, Maria

	yes	no
UNDERSTAND	☒	☐
SPEAK	☒	☐
READ	☒	☐
WRITE	☐	☒

CLASS LEVEL 3

ENGLISH SKILLS

NAME Cruz, Martin

	yes	no
UNDERSTAND	☒	☐
SPEAK	☒	☐
READ	☒	☐
WRITE	☐	☒

CLASS LEVEL 3

4. you / I

ENGLISH SKILLS

NAME _____

	yes	no
UNDERSTAND	☐	☐
SPEAK	☐	☐
READ	☐	☐
WRITE	☐	☐

CLASS LEVEL _____

C. **Listen and talk.**

a: Can you please **tell**
me the time?

give

b: **Yes, I can.**

No, sorry. I can't.

It's about 2:45.

Can you look at the clock in the
office?

a: **Thanks.**

Thank you.

b: **Welcome.**

Sure.

D. **Have conversations.**

EXAMPLE: 1. a: Can you tell me the time?
b: Yes, I can. It's 12:20.
a: Thanks.
b: Welcome.

1.

2.

3.

4.

5.

6.

7.

8.

the time now

Walk	south	three blocks	to Brown Road.
Don't turn	left		on First Avenue.
Go	straight	five blocks	on Green Boulevard.

E. Listen and talk.

a: Excuse me.
Can you please give me
directions to **the bus stop**?

a book store

b: Well, **I can try**.
Go **east** three blocks
to **School Street**.
Turn **left**.
Walk straight **north**.

all right
north
First Avenue
right
east

a: O.K. Three blocks **east**.
Turn **left** and
go **north**
to **the bus stop**.

north
right
east
the bookstore

b: **Yes**.

Right.

a: **Thanks a lot**.

Thank you.

b: **Welcome**.

Sure.

*F. Have conversations.

EXAMPLE: a: Excuse me. Can you give me directions to a telephone?
b: Well, walk north on First Avenue. Go two blocks to White Oak. Turn right
and go east to the telephone.

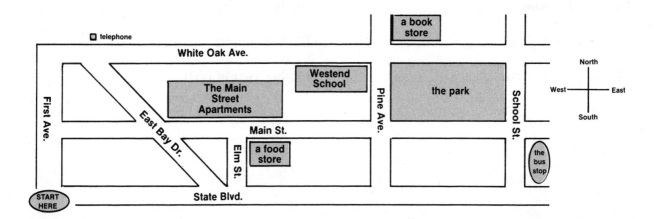

PART FOUR / READING AND WRITING

● Personal Information ● Signs

A. **Look and write the information on the lines.**

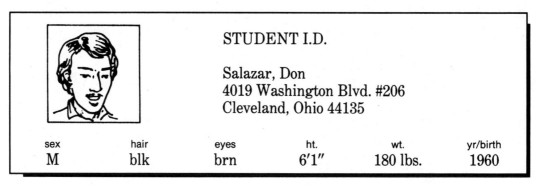

STUDENT I.D.

Salazar, Don
4019 Washington Blvd. #206
Cleveland, Ohio 44135

sex	hair	eyes	ht.	wt.	yr/birth
M	blk	brn	6'1"	180 lbs.	1960

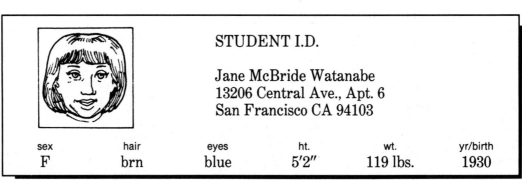

STUDENT I.D.

Jane McBride Watanabe
13206 Central Ave., Apt. 6
San Francisco CA 94103

sex	hair	eyes	ht.	wt.	yr/birth
F	brn	blue	5'2"	119 lbs.	1930

1. his first name ___Don___

2. his apartment number _____

3. his state _____

4. his sex _____

5. his hair color _____

6. his height _____

7. his year of birth _____

8. her last name _____

9. her street _____

10. her city _____

11. her zip code _____

12. her eye color _____

13. her weight _____

14. her year of birth _____

B. Look and write the heights and weights.

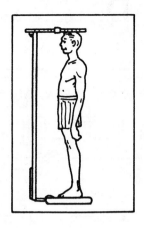

feet	+	inches	=	meters	+	centimeters
4'				1		22
4'		2"		1		27
4'		4"		1		32
4'		6"		1		37
4'		8"		1		42
4'		10"		1		47
5'				1		52
5'		2"		1		57
5'		4"		1		62
5'		6"		1		67
5'		8"		1		72
5'		10"		1		78
6'				1		85
6'		2"		1		88
6'		4"		1		93

pounds	=	kilograms
88		40
99		45
110		50
121		55
132		60
143		65
154		70
165		75
176		80
187		85
198		90
209		95
220		100

1. 1 meter 45 = __4__ ' __10__ "

2. 1 meter 52 = ___' ___"

3. 1 meter 78 = ___' ___"

4. 6 feet = ___ meter ___

5. 5 foot 6 = ___ meter ___

6. 5 foot 2 = ___ meter ___

7. 45 kilograms = __99__ pounds

8. 60 kilograms = ___ pounds

9. 95 kilograms = ___ pounds

10. 176 pounds = ___ kilograms

11. 143 pounds = ___ kilograms

12. 110 pounds = ___ kilograms

C. Print the information about you.

NAME _____ YEAR OF BIRTH _____

SEX _____ HT. _____ WT. _____ HAIR _____ EYES _____

D. Look and write the letters *A–H*.

1. __F__ Don't go left on this street.

2. ____ You can eat here now.

3. ____ You can buy this car.

4. ____ You can get the bus at this place.

5. ____ You can ask questions at this place.

6. ____ Don't go in here.

7. ____ Don't put your car here.

8. ____ Drive out here.

CHAPTER

4

Food and Money

COMPETENCIES:
Doing simple math (addition and multiplication)
Expressing needs and wants
Ordering food
Asking for and giving change
Understanding price lists
Reading signs

GRAMMAR FOCUS:
The simple present
Some and *any*
Object pronouns

We need to get some food.

PART ONE / VOCABULARY

● Food ● Math with Money ● Coins and Bills

A. Look and write the letters A–J.

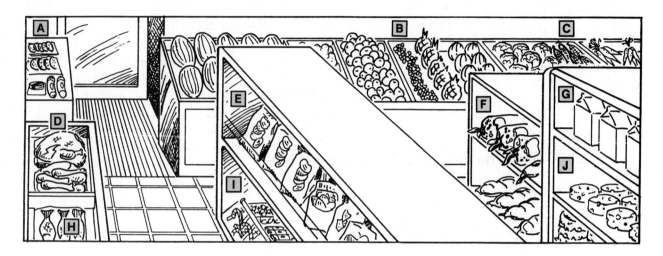

1. _F_ bread

2. ___ chicken

3. ___ lunch meat

4. ___ fish

5. ___ milk

6. ___ cheese

7. ___ fruit

8. ___ vegetables

9. ___ potato chips

10. ___ candy

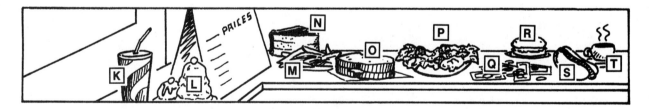

Look and write the letters K–T.

11. ___ a hamburger

12. ___ a hot dog

13. ___ a sandwich

14. ___ french fries

15. ___ a salad

16. ___ ice cream

17. ___ cake

18. ___ a soft drink

19. ___ a cup of coffee

20. ___ money (bills and change)

Math

5	+	30	+	21	=	56
Five	plus	thirty	plus	twenty-one	equals	fifty-six.

400	x	2	=	800
Four hundred	times	two	equals	eight hundred.

200	Two hundred		25	Twenty-five
+ 11	plus eleven		× 3	times three
211	is two (hundred) eleven.		75	is seventy-five.

B. **Write the answers. Then read the math.**

1.
```
   25
 + 10
 ————
   35
```

2.
```
   50
 +  5
 ————
```

3.
```
  100
 + 20
 ————
```

4.
```
  200
 + 45
 ————
```

5.
```
  400
 +106
 ————
```

6.
```
   50
   25
 + 13
 ————
```

7.
```
   10
   85
 +  1
 ————
```

8.
```
  100
   18
 + 80
 ————
```

9.
```
  500
  300
 +600
 ————
```

10.
```
   20
  350
 +815
 ————
```

11.
```
    8
  × 6
  ————
   48
```

12.
```
   50
  × 3
  ————
```

13.
```
   25
  × 4
  ————
```

14.
```
  400
  × 7
  ————
```

15.
```
  330
  × 2
  ————
```

Money (coins and bills)

$4
four dollars

$ .35
thirty-five
cents

$13.90
thirteen dollars and ninety cents
(thirteen ninety)

a penny

1¢ = $ .01
one cent

a nickel

5¢ = $ .05
five cents

a dime

10¢ = $ .10
ten cents

a quarter

25¢ = $ .25
twenty-five
cents

a dollar bill
(a one)

$1 = $1.00
one dollar

a five-dollar bill
(a five)

$5 = $5.00
five dollars

a ten-dollar bill
(a ten)

$10 = $10.00
ten dollars

a twenty-dollar bill
(a twenty)

$20 = $20.00
twenty dollars

C. Circle two letters.

1.

   (a.) two quarters
   b. $2.25
   (c.) $ .50
   d. $25.25

2.

   a. a ten and a five
   b. a dime and a nickel
   c. 15¢
   d. $15

3.

   a. two one-dollar bills
   b. a two-dollar bill
   c. $ .20
   d. $2.00

4.

   a. a fifteen-dollar
      bill
   b. a one and a five
   c. $15
   d. $6.00

5.

   a. a ten and two
      pennies
   b. ten oh two
   c. 10 × 2
   d. $2.10

6.

   a. a quarter, a dime,
      and a nickel
   b. forty pennies
   c. 40¢
   d. $40.00

Math with Money

$1.00	One dollar	
.50	plus fifty cents (two quarters: 25 x 2)	
.30	plus thirty cents (three dimes: 10 x 3)	
.05	plus five cents (one nickel)	
+ .02	plus two cents (two pennies)	
Total $1.87	is one dollar eighty-seven cents.	

D. Write the numbers for the money and the answers.

1. . _25_

  + . _10_

  = . _35_

2. . _____

  + . _____ (1 x 5)

  = . _____

3. _____.00

  + _____.00

  = _____.00

4. _____.00

  + _____ . _____

  _____ . _____

5. _____.00

  _____.00

  + _____.00

  = _____.00

6. . _____ (25 x 2)

  . _____

  + . _____ (5 x 3)

  = . _____

7. _____ . _____

  _____ . _____ (10 x 2)

  _____ . _____ (10 x 5)

  + _____ . _____ (5 x 4)

  = _____ . _____

the money
with you

*8. _____ . _____

  _____ . _____

  _____ . _____

  + _____ . _____

  = _____ . _____

PART TWO / LISTENING

● Needs and Wants

 A. **Listen and write the numbers _1–4_.**

B. **Listen and circle the pictures.**

1.

2.

 C. **Listen and follow the instructions.**

1. Check (✓) five lines.

_____	a hot dog
✓	a hamburger
_____	a chicken sandwich
_____	french fries
_____	a salad
_____	milk
_____	a soft drink
_____	cake
_____	ice cream

2. Write the numbers.

chicken sandwich	2.50
hot dog	_____.___
coffee	.50
milk	.____
tax	.37
TOTAL $	_____.___

PART THREE / GRAMMAR IN CONVERSATION

● The Simple Present ● *Some* and *Any* ● Object Pronouns
● Needs and Wants ● Change

I	want		coffee.		I		want		money.
We	need	(some)	vegetables.		We	don't	need	(any)	change.
They	have		hot dogs.		They		have		fruit.

 A. **Listen and talk.**

1. a: I want some **candy**.   coffee

   b: But we don't have any **money**.   time

2. a: We need some **fruit**.   bread

   b: They don't have any **fruit**.   bread

      Let's buy some **vegetables**.   cake

   a: But we don't need any **vegetables**.   cake
      We have enough.

3. a: We have some **hamburger meat**.   fruit

   b: But we **don't have enough** milk.   need some

   a: I want some **bread**.   hot dogs

   b: And let's get **a cake**.   ice cream

B. **Have conversations.**

EXAMPLE: **a:** We have enough hot dogs.
           b: But we don't have any vegetables.

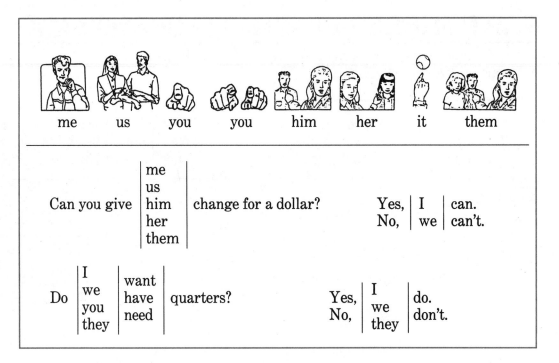

| me | us | you | you | him | her | it | them |

| Can you give | me
us
him
her
them | change for a dollar? | | Yes,
No, | I
we | can.
can't. |

| Do | I
we
you
they | want
have
need | quarters? | | Yes,
No, | I
we
they | do.
don't. |

Excuse me. Can you give me change for a five dollar bill?

Sorry, I don't have it, but you can ask him.

C. Listen and talk.

1. a: Excuse me. Can you
       please give **me** change   us
       for a **five**-dollar bill?   ten

    b: Sorry. I **don't have it**.   can't
       But you can ask **him**.   her

2. a: **Can I have** change   Do you have
       for a **five**, please?   one

    b: **Yes, you can.**   Let's see.
       Four ones,   Fifty cents
       two quarters,   a quarter
       and **five dimes.**   five nickels

D. Have conversations.

EXAMPLE: **a:** Can I please have change for a twenty?
b: Let's see. Yes, I have a ten-dollar bill and two fives.

1.  =

2.  =

3.  =

4.  =

5.  =

6. =

*7.  =

*8.  =

*E. Ask and give change with your money.

PART FOUR / READING AND WRITING

● Price Lists ● Math Signs

LUNCH MENU

	Prices		Prices
hamburger	2.25	cake	.95
hot dog	1.50	soft drinks	
chicken sandwich	2.10	large	.80
salad	1.20	small	.60
french fries	1.00	coffee	.75
ice cream	.80	milk	.85

A. Look and write the prices from the menu.

1. french fries $ __1__ . __00__

2. cake $ __.95__

3. milk $ ____ . _____

4. two hot dogs $ ____ . _____

5. three hamburgers $ ____ . _____

6. a small soft drink $ ____ . _____

7. six large soft drinks $ ____ . _____

8. two cups of coffee $ ____ . _____

B. Write the prices from the menu and the answers.

1.

1 hamburger	2 . 25
1 chicken sandwich	2 . 10
1 small soft drink	. 60
tax	. 25
TOTAL $	5 . 20

2.

2 hot dogs	____ . ____
1 salad	____ . ____
1 coffee	____ . ____
tax	. 30
TOTAL $	____ . ____

3.

2 hamburgers	_____ . _____
1 chicken sandwich	_____ . _____
2 french fries	_____ . _____
1 salad	_____ . _____
tax	. 49
TOTAL $	_____ . _____

4.

4 hot dogs	_____ . _____
5 salads	_____ . _____
5 ice cream	_____ . _____
5 small soft drinks	_____ . _____
tax	1. 50
TOTAL $	_____ . _____

*C. **Write some kinds of food from the menu. Write the prices and the total.**

1.

	CHECK	
AMT	DESCRIPTION	PRICE
1	hamburger	2.25
	TOTAL	

2.

	CHECK	
AMT	DESCRIPTION	PRICE
	TOTAL	

D. Look and write the letters *A–H*.

1. __B__   You can take food home from this restaurant.

2. ____   This morning meal isn't expensive.

3. ____   You can eat here at any time.

4. ____   Here are the hours of this restaurant.

5. ____   You can't sit at a table for lunch.

6. ____   You pay cash at this store.

7. ____   You get drinks with your lunch.

8. ____   You can save money at this market.

Times and Places

COMPETENCIES:
Reading and telling the time, day, and date
Describing the weather
Expressing location
Making social appointments
Reading calendars
Reading thermometers and weather maps
Understanding time zones

GRAMMAR FOCUS:
Wh-questions with *be*
It's and *there's*

It's windy and cold today.

PART ONE / VOCABULARY

● Places and Locations ● Time, Days, Months, and Dates ● Weather

A. Check (√) the true sentences. $\boxed{\text{in}}$ $\overset{\text{on}}{\boxed{}}$ next to $\boxed{}$

1. _√_ There's a bank in this shopping center.

2. ____ There's a snack bar there, too.

3. ____ There's a post office next to the bank.

4. ____ There's a coffee shop next to the post office.

5. ____ There's a bookstore on the first level.

6. ____ There's a drugstore on the second level.

7. ____ There's no library in this shopping center.

8. ____ But you can go to a clothing store and a food store there.

B. Look and write the numbers of the pictures.

1. _2_ The temperature is 23 degrees Fahrenheit (–4 degrees Centigrade). It's very cold.

2. _____ It's very hot. It's over 100 degrees.

3. _____ It's a warm, sunny day. It's not windy or cold.

4. _____ It's a cloudy day. But there's no rain.

5. _____ It's Monday. It's late in the afternoon.

6. _____ What day is it? It's the twenty-sixth of July.

7. _____ It's the last month of the year.

8. _____ It's early in the day. It's morning.

Days, Months, and Dates

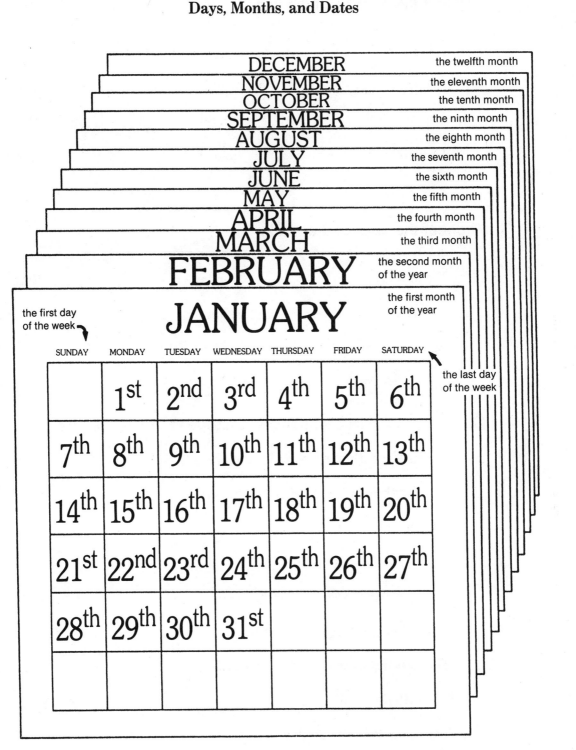

DECEMBER	the twelfth month
NOVEMBER	the eleventh month
OCTOBER	the tenth month
SEPTEMBER	the ninth month
AUGUST	the eighth month
JULY	the seventh month
JUNE	the sixth month
MAY	the fifth month
APRIL	the fourth month
MARCH	the third month
FEBRUARY	the second month of the year
JANUARY	the first month of the year

the first day of the week

the last day of the week

SUNDAY	MONDAY	TUESDAY	WEDNESDAY	THURSDAY	FRIDAY	SATURDAY
	1st	2nd	3rd	4th	5th	6th
7th	8th	9th	10th	11th	12th	13th
14th	15th	16th	17th	18th	19th	20th
21st	22nd	23rd	24th	25th	26th	27th
28th	29th	30th	31st			

What's the date today?   It's January twenty-second. =
It's the twenty-second of January.

It's August sixteenth. =
It's the sixteenth of August.

C. Number the months of the year.

| 1 – 12 |

____ March	__1__ January	____ September
____ October	____ April	__2__ February
____ July	____ November	____ May
____ December	____ June	____ August

D. Number the days of the week.

| 1 – 7 |

____ Wednesday	____ Monday	____ Saturday
____ Tuesday	____ Friday	____ Thursday
__1__ Sunday		

E. Check (√) the true sentences. Change the wrong words.

1. __√__ The first month of the year is January.

2. ____ The fourth month is ~~March~~. April

3. ____ The seventh month is August.

4. ____ October is the tenth month.

5. ____ February is the second month.

6. ____ November is the twelfth month.

7. ____ The first day of the week is Sunday.

8. ____ The fifth day is Wednesday.

9. ____ The third day is Thursday.

10. ____ The sixth day is Friday.

PART TWO / LISTENING

● Time and Dates ● Location ● Weather

 A. **Listen and write the numbers _1–4_.**

B. **Listen and write the words and numbers.**

Monday	Thursday	Friday	November	December

5	30	405

1.

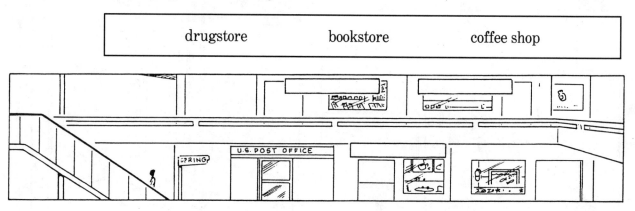

2.

CLASS CARD
Level 2

_____ , _Wednesday_ , _____

Time: _1_ : _____ to 3:45

First class: January _____

Room: _____

 C. **Listen and follow the instructions.**

1. Write the places on the signs.

drugstore	bookstore	coffee shop

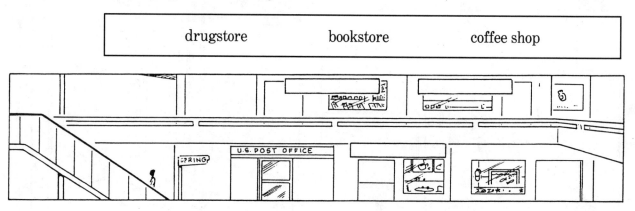

2. Circle the temperature and one picture. Put X on two pictures.

PART THREE / GRAMMAR IN CONVERSATION

● *Wh*-Questions with *Be* ● *It's* and *There's*
● The Time, Day, and Dates ● The Weather ● Appointments and Locations

What's	your name?	what's	= what is
Who's	your teacher?	who's	= who is
Where's	the restroom?	where's	= where is
When's	your class?	when's	= when is

 A. **Listen and talk.**

a: Do you like **your class**?   to study English

b: **Yes, I do.**   No, I don't.

a: **Who's** your teacher?   What's the name of

b: **Martin Kline.**   Mary York.

a: Where's the **class**?   classroom

b: It's **in Room 360**.   at Evans School

a: **When's** the class?   What day is

b: On **Monday and Wednesday**.   Tuesdays

a: What time is **the class**?   it

b: It's at **9:00 in the morning**.   6:30 in the evening

a: How much is **the class**?   it

b: It's ten dollars for **books**.   a student card

a: Can I **take** a class, too?   go to

b: I don't know. **Talk to the teacher.**   You can ask in the office.

*B. **Work together. Ask the questions in A. Answer them.**

EXAMPLE: a: Do you like your English class?
          b: Yes, I do.
          a: Who's your teacher?

| What time | is | it | (now)? | It's | (about) 10:45. |
| What day | is | it | (today)? | It's | Tuesday, September 11. |

| | Is | it | late?
cloudy?
a nice day? | | Yes,
No, | it is.
it's not. |

C. Listen and talk.

1. a: **What time is it**?   Can you tell me the time?

b: I think it's about **7:30**.   3:15

a: **What day of the week is it**?   What's the date?

b: It's **Saturday**.   May 2

2. a: Is it a nice **day** today?   afternoon

b: **Yes, it is**.   No, it's not.
It's **warm and sunny**.   windy and cold

D. Have conversations.

EXAMPLE: **1. a:** What time is it now?
b: It's 2:10.
a: What day is it?

1.

2.

3.

*4.

the time now   the date today   the weather

E.　**Listen and talk.**

a:　**Do you want to**　　　　　Let's
　　get together?　　　　　　study together.

b:　Sure. **When?**　　　　　　What day?

a:　Is today **all right**?　　　　good for you

b:　No, sorry, **it's not.**　　　　I can't today
　　How about Saturday?　　　What about

a:　O.K. **What time?**　　　　　When?

b:　At **lunchtime**?　　　　　　3:30

a:　**Good**.　　　　　　　　　Sure.

*F.　**Talk to some classmates. When can you meet? Write their names and times in some boxes.**

EXAMPLE:　a:　Can we get together this week?
　　　　　b:　All right. What day is good for you?
　　　　　a:　How about this Wednesday?
　　　　　b:　O.K. Is 2:00 a good time?
　　　　　a:　Yes, it is. Let's write it on our calendars.

	Sunday	Monday	Tuesday	Wednesday	Thursday	Friday	Saturday
10:00							
12:00							
2:00							
4:00							
6:00							
8:00							

		on State Street.
There's	a restaurant	on the first level.
		next to the bank.

		in the shopping center?
Is there	a coffee shop	on this street?
		there?

G. Listen and talk.

a: There's a shopping center
on **Fifth Street**.   Pine Avenue
Can you meet me   Let's meet
at the **restaurant**?   coffee shop.

b: **O.K.** Where is it?   All right.

a: It's on the **second** level.   first

b: Is there a **drugstore**   a bank
in the shopping center, too?   there

a: **Yes, there is**. It's next to   Uh-huh.
the **restaurant**.   coffee shop

*H. Talk with the classmates on your calendar in F. Where can you meet? Write the names of places in the boxes.

EXAMPLE: **a:** We can get together at 7:30 on Thursday. Where?
b: There's a library on Central Avenue. Can we meet there?
a: O.K. Where is it?
b: It's next to the post office.

PART FOUR / READING AND WRITING

● The Calendar and Dates ● Weather Maps and Thermometers ● Time Zones

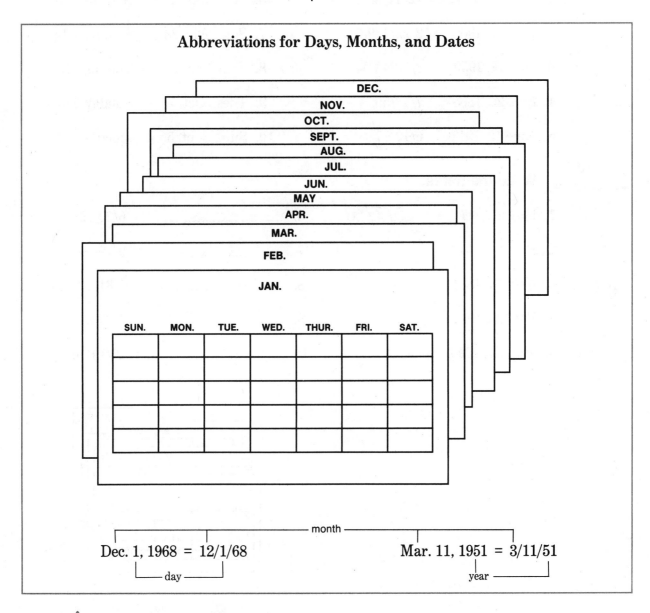

Abbreviations for Days, Months, and Dates

Dec. 1, 1968 = 12/1/68

Mar. 11, 1951 = 3/11/51

A. Write the abbreviations.

1. Friday   Fri.   7. Thursday   _____   13. August   _____

2. Wednesday   _____   8. January   _____   14. November   _____

3. Monday   _____   9. April   _____   15. March   _____

4. Sunday   _____   10. February   _____   16. September   _____

5. Saturday   _____   11. October   _____

6. Tuesday   _____   12. December   _____

_____ **B.** **Match the dates.**

1. Aug. 30, 1943   12/11/68
2. Dec. 11, 1968   2/22/1898
3. July 18, 1959   8/30/43
4. Feb. 22, 1898   7/18/59
5. June 12, 1917   6/12/17

6. Mon., Jan. 1   Saturday, 3/23
7. Sat., Mar. 23   Friday, 4/14
8. Fri., Apr. 14   Tuesday, 10/7
9. Tues., Oct. 7   Sunday, 9/5
10. Sun., Sept. 5   Monday, 1/1

_____ **C.** **Write the dates.**

1. May 2, 1947   = _5/2/47_   6. _____ = 6/20/45
2. Dec. 1, 1968   = _____   7. _____ = 9/19/50
3. Nov. 14, 1881 = _____   8. _____ = 1/31
4. Feb. 23, 1917 = _____   9. _____ = 4/26/31
5. Mar. 17, 1995 = _____   10. _____ = 10/10/10

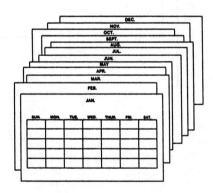

_____ **D.** **Write the days and the dates.**

	day of the week	month	day	year
1. today	_____ ,	_____	_____ ,	_____
2. your birth	_____ ,	_____	_____ ,	_____
3. the first day of class	_____ ,	_____	_____ ,	_____
4. the last day of class	_____ ,	_____	_____ ,	_____

E. Look and write the times.

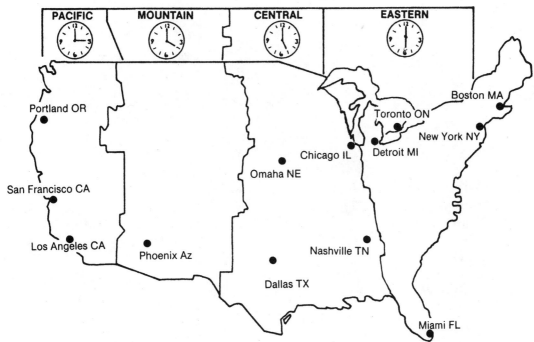

CITY STATE	TIME		CITY STATE	TIME
1. Los Angeles, California	3:00		4. Miami, Florida	_____
2. Boston, Massachusetts	_____		5. Dallas, Texas	_____
3. Portland, Oregon	_____		6. Chicago, Illinois	_____

*F. Write the time now.

1. in your city	_____		5. in Phoenix, Arizona	_____
2. in Detroit, Michigan	_____		6. in San Francisco, California	_____
3. in New York, New York	_____		7. in Omaha, Nebraska	_____
4. in Toronto, Ontario	_____		8. in Nashville, Tennessee	_____

G. Look and write about the weather.

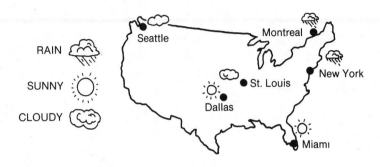

CITY	STATE/PROVINCE	WEATHER
1. Dallas, Texas		sunny
2. Miami, Florida		
3. St. Louis, Missouri		
4. Seattle, Washington		
5. Montreal, Quebec		
6. New York, New York		

H. Look and write the temperatures.

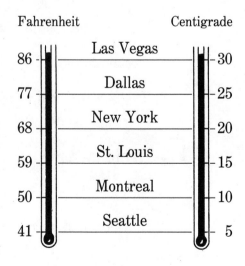

CITY	TEMPERATURE	
	Fahrenheit	Centigrade
1. St. Louis	59	15
2. Las Vegas		
3. Seattle		
4. Montreal		
5. Dallas		
6. New York		

*I. Write about the weather and the temperature in your city today.

1. The weather today is _____ .

2. The temperature is _____ degrees Fahrenheit and _____ degrees Centigrade.

The Body

COMPETENCIES:
Telling clothing sizes and prices
Describing physical feelings, illnesses, and
   health habits
Understanding and filling out medical forms
Reading medicine labels

GRAMMAR FOCUS:
The verb *be*
Frequency words

What's the matter? I'm sick.

PART ONE / VOCABULARY

● Body Parts ● Clothing and Things ● Physical Feelings and Illnesses

A. Write the letters *A–I* on the lines.

1. __E__ his nose

2. ____ his eyes

3. ____ his head

4. ____ his shoulder

5. ____ his chest

6. ____ his shirt

7. ____ jeans (pants)

8. ____ a hat

9. ____ a jacket

B. Write the *J–U* letters on the lines.

10. __T__ her leg

11. ____ her heart

12. ____ her back

13. ____ her ear

14. ____ her stomach

15. ____ a blouse

16. ____ a long skirt

17. ____ a big sweater

18. ____ wide shoes (not tight)

19. ____ tablets and capsules

20. ____ a teaspoon for medicine

21. ____ a glass of water

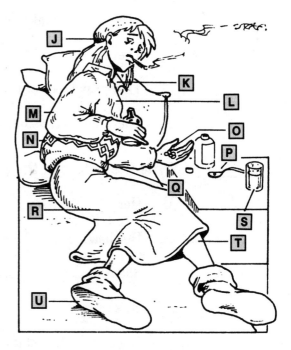

C. Write the numbers of the pictures *1–2*.

1. __1__ The mother and father aren't well. They feel terrible.

2. _____ The children aren't sick or tired. They feel fine.

3. _____ They need to make an appointment with the doctor.

4. _____ They're worried about their health and medical bills.

5. _____ They're not too cold or too hot.

6. _____ They don't have stomachaches or headaches.

D. Write the letters of the people *A–D*.

1. __B__ Her throat is sore.

2. _____ Her head is hot. She has a fever (a temperature of 102°).

3. _____ She isn't sick to her stomach. She's hungry.

4. _____ He's thirsty.

5. _____ His nose is stuffed up.

6. _____ His ears hurt.

PART TWO / LISTENING

- Clothing Sizes and Prices ● Physical Feelings and Illnesses ● Health Habits
- Medical Instructions

 A. **Listen and write the numbers.**

B. **Listen and follow the instructions.**

1. Match the clothing with the sizes and the prices.

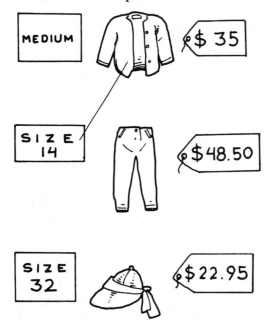

MEDIUM

ϕ $ 35

S I Z E
14

ϕ $48.50

S I Z E
32

ϕ $22.95

2. Check ✓ the four problems.

☐ a headache

✓ a sore throat

☐ a toothache

☐ a stuffed-up nose

☐ a stomachache

☐ a fever (a temperature over 98.6 degrees)

☐ an earache

3. Put ✕ in the boxes.

Do you	always	sometimes	never		always	sometimes	never
smoke?	☐	✕	☐	eat well?	☐	☐	☐
drink alcohol?	☐	☐	☐	exercise?	☐	☐	☐

4. Write the words.

capsules	tablet	meal
morning	alcohol	milk

Take 1 _____ before

every _____ . Don't

drink any _____ .

Take 2 _____ every

_____ and afternoon.

Don't drink _____ with them.

PART THREE / GRAMMAR IN CONVERSATION

- The Verb *Be* • Frequency Words
- Describing Clothing Sizes • Describing Physical Feelings, Illnesses, and Health Habits

	yes			no		
1	The hat The dress	is	too small.	The jacket The skirt	isn't	big enough.
2+	The shoes The jeans	are	too wide. just right.	The pants The shirts	aren't	the right size.

A. **Listen and talk.**

a: The **hat is** just right.   shirts are

b: But the **jacket**   sweater
is too **big**.   small

a: And the **jeans**   pants
aren't **long** enough.   tight

B. **Make sentences.**

EXAMPLE: **1. a.** The skirt is just right.
b. But the hat is too big.
c. And the shoes aren't big enough.

1.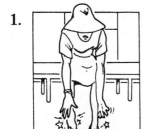

2.

3.

4.

5.

*6.

your clothing

	yes			no	
1	I	'm		I'm not	
	You	're	sick.	You aren't	tired.
	He	's		He isn't	
	She	's		She isn't	
2+	We	're		We	
	You	're	cold.	You	aren't	worried.
	They	're		They	

I'm	=	I am		
he's	=	he is	he isn't	=	he's not
she's	=	she is	she isn't	=	she's not
we're	=	we are	we aren't	=	we're not
you're	=	you are	you aren't	=	you're not
they're	=	they are	they aren't	=	they're not

 C.   **Listen and talk.**

1. **a:** **I want to make** an appointment   Can I make
   with Dr. Ito, **please.**   please?
   I **don't feel well.**   feel terrible

   b: What's the **problem**?   matter

   a: I'm **sick to my stomach.**   very tired
   And my **temperature** is   shoulder
   102 degrees.   sore

2. **a:** **My sister is** sick, too.   Our children are

   b: **What's the matter**?   What's wrong?

   a: **She's** very warm.   They're
   And **she isn't** hungry.   they aren't

D.   Have conversations.

EXAMPLE: **1. a:** What's the problem?
          b: She's sick to her stomach. And her throat is sore.

1. she / her

> PROBLEMS
>
> sick to her stomach
> throat—sore

2. I / my

> PROBLEMS
>
> very tired
> temperature—103°F

3. he / his

> PROBLEMS
>
> not hungry
> nose—stuffed up

4. we / our

> PROBLEMS
>
> very cold
> hands—not warm

5. they / their

> PROBLEMS
>
> very thirsty
> heads—hot

*6. I

> PROBLEMS
>
> your problems

Are	you / they	very tired?	Yes,	I am. / we they are.	No,	I'm not. / we they aren't.
Is	he / she	thirsty?	Yes,	he / she is.	No,	he / she isn't.

E.   Listen and talk.

a: **Are you** very sick?   Are your children

b: Yes, **I am.**   they are

a: Can you come in
this afternoon   this morning
at **5:15**?   9:45

b: That's **too late**.   too early for us

a: Is 3:30 **a good time**?   all right

b: **That's fine**. Thanks.   It's just right.

a: **Your name**, please?   Their names

F.   Have conversations.

EXAMPLE: 1.   **a:** Is 1:00 on Monday all right for him?
  b: No, sorry. It isn't.
  a: Then how about 11:30 on Tuesday morning?
  b: That's fine. Thanks.
  a: And his name, please?
  b: It's Martin Cruz.

1.

```
APPOINTMENT

For   Martin Cruz

    M   (T)   W   T   F

at  11:30  in the  (morning.)
                    afternoon.
```

2.

```
APPOINTMENT

For   Jane Yun

    M   T   W   T   (F)

at  9:45  in the  (morning.)
                   afternoon.
```

3.

```
APPOINTMENT

For   Abdul Aziz

    M   T   (W)   T   F

at  3:20  in the  morning.
                  (afternoon.)
```

*4.

```
APPOINTMENT

For  _____
          (your name)
    M   T   W   T   F

at  _____  in the  morning.
                      afternoon.
```

I	never / usually / always	exercise in the morning.	I'm	sometimes / often / always	tired.
Do you	ever / sometimes	take medicine?	Are you	ever / often	sick?

 **G.** **Listen and talk.**

1. **a:** I usually **eat well**.   drink water
   But I'm always **hungry**.   thirsty

   b: Do you **eat**   drink
   three meals   eight glasses
   every day?   a day

   a: <u>**Yes, I do**</u>.   No, I don't.

2. **a:** Are you **ever sick**?   often tired

   b: Yes, **sometimes**.   usually

   a: Do you usually
   take medicine?   try to sleep

   b: <u>**No, I don't**</u>.   Sometimes.

H. **Check (✓) boxes and have conversations.**

EXAMPLE: **a:** Are you tired now?
           b: Yes, I am. I'm often tired.
           a: Do you ever smoke?
           b: Yes, I do. I sometimes smoke after meals.

Name _____		never	sometimes	often	always
Are you	tired?	☐	☐	☐	☐
	hungry?	☐	☐	☐	☐
	very thirsty?	☐	☐	☐	☐
	worried?	☐	☐	☐	☐
	sick?	☐	☐	☐	☐
Do you	smoke?	☐	☐	☐	☐
	drink alcohol?	☐	☐	☐	☐
	eat well?	☐	☐	☐	☐
	exercise?	☐	☐	☐	☐
	take medicine?	☐	☐	☐	☐

PART FOUR / READING AND WRITING

● Medical Forms ● Medicine Labels

A. Look and write the information.

Name of patient _Billy Ross_____

Who's responsible for the bills? _Mr. James Ross (father)_____

Medical insurance _The Goodcare Company_____

Past Diseases	Immunizations	Operations	Dates
measles	D P T	tonsils	11/5/82
mumps	polio		

Do you have   Do you often have

	yes	no			yes	no
eye problems?		✓		headaches?		✓
heart problems?		✓		earaches?	✓	
backaches?		✓		sore throats?	✓	
stomachaches?	✓			a fever?		✓

1. the name of the patient _____

2. the person responsible for his bills _____

3. the name of his health insurance company _____

4. his past diseases _____   _____

5. his immunizations _____   _____

6. his operation _____   the date _____

7. his health problems _____   _____

_____

*B. Write and check (√) the information about you.

Name of patient _____

Who's responsible for the bills? _____

Medical insurance _____

Past Diseases	Immunizations	Operations	Dates
_____	_____	_____	_____
_____	_____	_____	_____

Do you have   Do you often have

	yes	no			yes	no
eye problems?	☐	☐		headaches?	☐	☐
heart problems?	☐	☐		earaches?	☐	☐
backaches?	☐	☐		sore throats?	☐	☐
stomachaches?	☐	☐		a fever?	☐	☐

C. Look and write the letters *A–F*.

A
No. 102-810   Dr. Bass
Billy Ross   5/14/88

Take one teaspoon at
bedtime.

B
No. 10590   Dr. Gomez
Chang Lee   7/6/89

Take 1 tablet 3 times
a day with food.

C
Use on skin
once or twice
every day.

D
Put 2 drops
in each ear
every morning
evening.

E
Spray into nose
no more than
5 times a day.

F
2 capsules
after every meal.

Do not drink alcohol.

1. ☐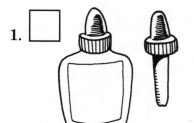

2. ☐

3. ☐

4. ☐

5. ☐

6. ☐

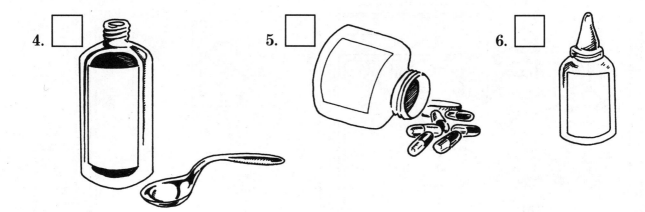

People

COMPETENCIES:
Locating countries on a world map
Recognizing family relationships
Recognizing job titles and work descriptions
Using the post office
Giving and taking telephone messages
Asking and telling about relatives and friends
Addressing envelopes
Understanding postal and telephone information

GRAMMAR FOCUS:
Possessive nouns
The simple present: -s forms

My family lives in Iraq.

PART ONE / VOCABULARY

• Location of Countries   • Family Relationships   • Job Titles and Work

A. **Look and check (√) the true sentences on page 92.**

1. ____ China is northeast of Japan.

2. __✓__ It's next to India and Vietnam.

3. ____ Australia is in the Atlantic Ocean.

4. ____ There are five big countries in North America.

5. ____ Brazil is in Central America.

6. ____ Peru is west of Brazil. Argentina is south of Brazil.

7. ____ France is between Spain and Germany.

8. ____ Iran is between Libya and Turkey.

9. ____ Nigeria and Ethiopia are in the Middle East.

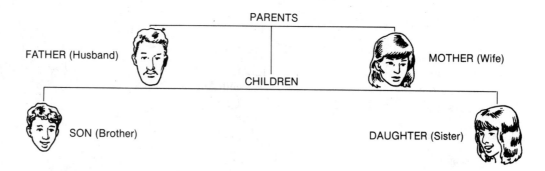

B. Circle the words.

1. My father and │ mother / sister │ are my parents.

2. My │ brother / husband │ is my mother's son.

3. My brother's │ wife / friend │ is my relative, too.

4. Their │ brother / son │ and daughter are their children.

5. My │ wife / sister │ is my father's daughter.

6. My sister and her │ husband / brother │ have two children.

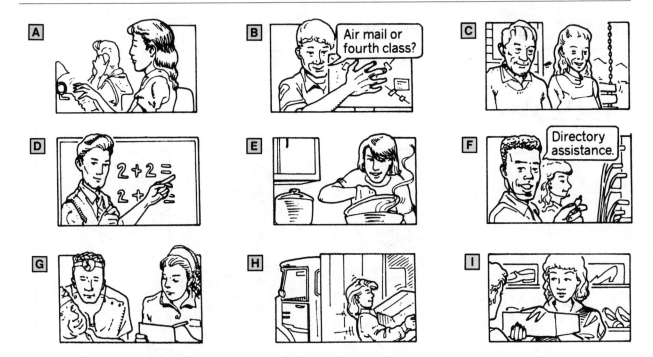

C. **Look and write the letters. Then match the words.**

1. _C_ Retired people — type and take messages in offices.

2. ___ A teacher — weighs mail (packages and letters) and sells stamps.

3. ___ A postal worker — don't work at jobs.

4. ___ Secretaries — teaches in a school.

5. ___ A housewife or housekeeper — cooks and cleans the house.

6. ___ A truck driver — give information and dial numbers.

7. ___ A salesclerk — take care of patients.

8. ___ Doctors and nurses — drives and delivers things.

9. ___ Telephone operators — sells things in a store or shop.

PART TWO / LISTENING

● The Post Office ● Countries ● Telephone Messages ● Job Titles and Descriptions

 A. **Listen and write the numbers *1–4*.**

B. **Listen and follow the instructions.**

1. Circle three pictures.

· **2.** Write the names of the countries on the map.

| Panama | Guatemala | Nicaragua |

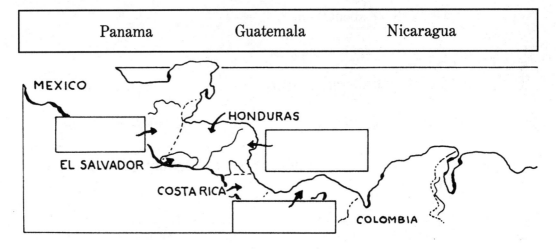

3. Circle the words.

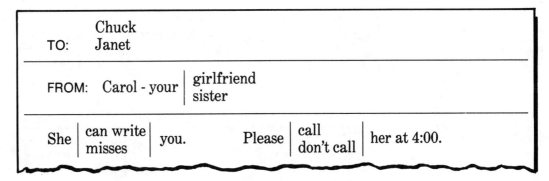

4. Match the words.

She   sells clothing in a men's store.

He   drives a truck.

His wife   is a waitress in a coffee shop.

Her husband   is a salesclerk in a drugstore.

PART THREE /GRAMMAR IN CONVERSATION

● Possessive Nouns ● The Simple Present: *-s* Forms
● Family Relationships ● Jobs and Work Descriptions ● Telephone Messages

My	mother's	name is Doris.
My	sister's	boyfriend is from Peru.
What's your	son's	name?
What are your	children's	names?

A. **Listen and talk.**

a: I miss my **family**.   friends

b: Oh? Tell me about them.

a: Well, my **sister's** name is Lee.   best friend's

b: What's your **brother's** name?   boyfriend's

a: I don't have a **brother**.   boyfriend

B. **Write the names of people in your family. (You can put ✕ for no name.)**

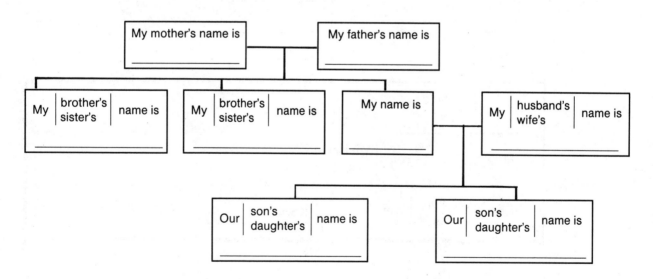

Ask and answer questions about the names of relatives.

EXAMPLE: **a:** What's your mother's name?
b: My mother's name is Fahimeh. What's your sister's name?
a: I don't have a sister. What are your children's names?

	I, you, 2+			**1**	
yes	I We You My sons	go to school.	My sister She Our father He	goes to school.
no	I We You My sons	don't type.	My sister She Our father He	doesn't type.

	Do	you	work?		Does	he	live with you?
Where	do	you	live?	Where	does	she	work?
What	do	they	do?	What	does	he	do?

 C. **Listen and talk.**

1. **a:** <u>I'm</u> from Argentina.
   Where are **you** from?

   b: <u>I'm</u> from Venezuela.

   My parents are
   your parents

   They're

2. **a:** <u>I</u> live in New York.

   Where do **you** live?

   b: <u>I</u> live in Los Angeles.
   Where does your **brother** live?

   a: <u>He</u> lives in London, England.

   My relatives

   your relatives

   They
   best friend

   She

3. **a:** <u>What do you do?</u>

   b: I'm a <u>housewife</u>.
   I <u>take care of children</u>.
   <u>How about you?</u>

   a: I work in a <u>restaurant</u>.

   Do you work?

   teacher
   teach English
   And you?

   coffee shop

4. a: What **does your father** do?   does your wife

   b: **He doesn't** work.   She doesn't
     He's retired.   She's a student.

5. a: Where does your **mother** work?   sister

   b: In **people's homes**.   a store
     She **cooks and cleans**.   sells things
     She's a **housekeeper**.   salesclerk

*D. Have conversations with two classmates. Write the answers.

EXAMPLE: a: Where are you from?
           b: The Philippines.
           a: Where do you work?
           b: In a hospital.
           a: What's your job?
           b: I take care of sick people. I'm a nurse.

	Classmate 1	Classmate 2
1. Where are you from?		
2. Where do you work?		
3. What do you do? (What's your job?)		
4. What's your | sister's / brother's / friend's / _____'s | name?		
5. Where does | he / she / he | live?		
6. What does she do?		

 **E.** **Listen and talk.**

    a: Hello.

    b: Hello. Is <u>Carol</u> there, please?   your father

    a: No, <u>**she isn't**</u>.   he's not
        <u>**Can I take a**</u> message?   Is there any

    b: Yes, <u>**you can.**</u>   there is
        Please tell <u>**her**</u>   him
        <u>**Chuck**</u>   Ann Smith
        <u>**can be there at 8:30.**</u>   needs her check today

    F. **Have "telephone conversations."**

EXAMPLE: **1. a:** Hello.
               b: Hello. Is Anthony there, please?
               a: No, he isn't. Is there any message?
               b: Yes. Please tell him his mother is sick. She needs some medicine.

1.

TELEPHONE MESSAGE
TO: _Anthony_
Your mother is sick.
She needs some
medicine.

2.

TELEPHONE MESSAGE
TO: _Hiroko_
Lee Sook can't come
to school this afternoon.
She needs her books.

3.

TELEPHONE MESSAGE
TO: _My Ling_
Your brother has to
work late. You can
call him at the office.

*4.

TELEPHONE MESSAGE
TO: _____
_____
_____
_____

PART FOUR / READING AND WRITING

● Envelopes and Postal Information ● Telephone Information

A. **Look and write the information.**

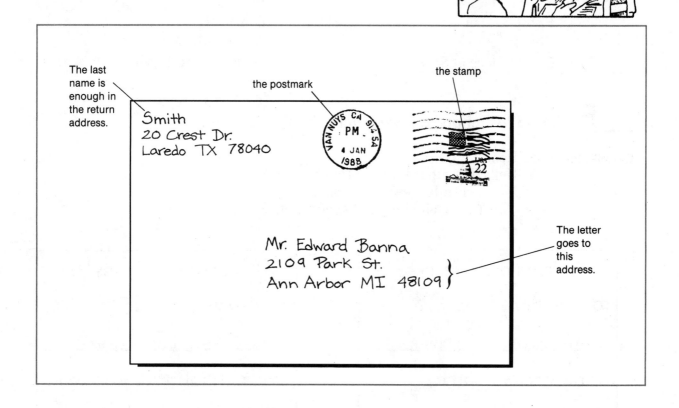

1. The date of the postmark is _____ , _____ _____ .
                                         month   day   year

2. The last name of the letter writer is _____ .

3. The letter comes from _____ , _____ .
                                    city   state

4. The letter goes to Mr. _____ _____ .
                                     first name   last name

5. The letter goes to _____ ,
                            number   street

   _____ , _____ _____ .
                     city   state   zip code

B. Address the envelopes.

1. It's from Sally Brown, 213 Elm St., Chicago IL 60613. It goes to Ms. Mary Yu, 31002 W. Bay Dr., Denver CO 10999.

```
_____
_____
_____

                    _____
                    _____
                    _____
```

*2. It's from you. It's to a classmate.

```
_____
_____
_____

                    _____
                    _____
                    _____
```

*3. It's from you to a friend or a person in your family.

```
_____
_____
_____

                    _____
                    _____
                    _____
```

C. Look and write the answers.

What time do they come for the mail?

Mail Collection Times FOR THIS BOX			
Mon. through Fri.		**Sunday**	
A.M	P.M.	A.M.	P.M.
[ ]	12:30	[ ]	[ ]
[ ]	4:30		
Saturday		**Holidays**	
A.M.	P.M.	A.M.	P.M.
11:00	[ ]	[ ]	[ ]

The Last Collection
in This Area
Is at

30th St. and Ocean Blvd.

For Additional
Collection Locations,
Please Call

555-1716

1. Does the mail truck come for the mail on Sunday? _____ No _____

2. Does it come for the mail on Monday morning? _____

3. Does it come for the mail on Tuesday afternoon? _____

4. How many times do they get the mail on Wednesday? _____

   What's the first time? _____ What's the last time? _____

5. How many times do they come for the mail on Saturday? _____

6. How many times do they get the mail on holidays? _____

7. Where can you take letters after 4:30 on Thursday? _____

   _____

8. What number can you call for the location of other mailboxes? _____

   _____

D. Look and write the answers.

COINS

This telephone number is
208 555-5671

This location is
2929 31st St.

5¢
10¢
25¢

LOCAL CALLS   20¢

Local and Station-to-Station Coin Paid Calls

Within this Area Code   Number
Outside this Area Code   1 + Area Code + Number

FREE CALLS

EMERGENCY   911
Directory Assistance   411
Operator   0

1. What's the number of this pay telephone? _____

2. At what address is this telephone? _____

3. How do you call a local number with the 208 area code? You

   dial the _____.

4. How do you call a number with the 307 area code? You dial

   _____ + _____ + the _____.

5. Does an emergency phone call cost money? _____

6. What's the number for an emergency call? _____

7. What's the number for the operator? _____

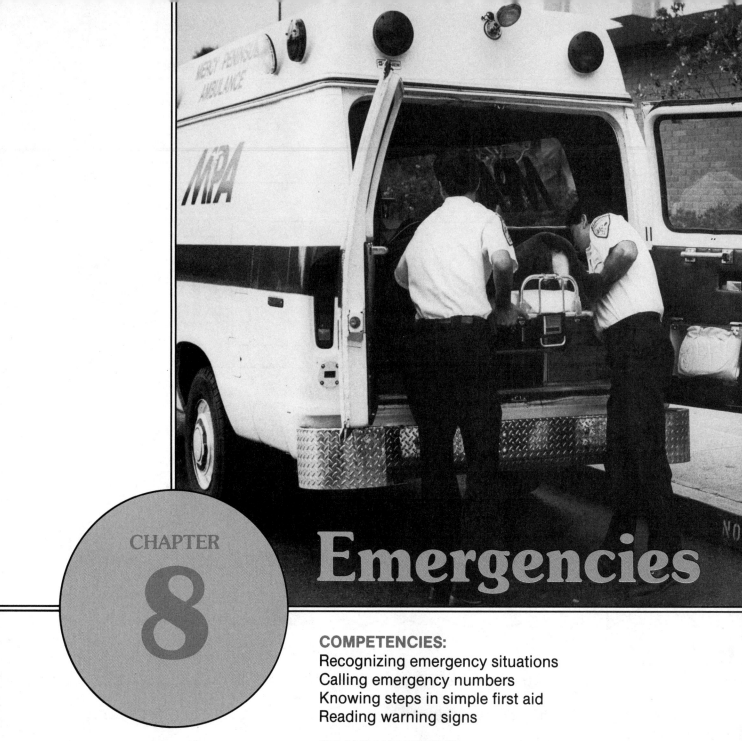

Emergencies

COMPETENCIES:
Recognizing emergency situations
Calling emergency numbers
Knowing steps in simple first aid
Reading warning signs

GRAMMAR FOCUS:
The present continuous

NOTE: The first aid instructions in this chapter are based on information in *A Sigh of Relief: the First-Aid Handbook for Childhood Emergencies*, produced by Martin Green, Bantam Books, Inc., 1977. However, because they are not complete, we recommend that readers take a first aid course and study books on the subject before attempting to follow the steps.

PART ONE / VOCABULARY

● Emergencies and First Aid

A. Look and write the letters A–G.

1. _E_   He's choking! He can't cough or breathe.

2. ____   I'm having a heart attack. I need the paramedics!

3. ____   I'm bleeding.

4. ____   He's drowning.

5. ____   It's smoke from a fire. When is the fire department coming?

6. ____   Someone is trying to break into the house! He's dangerous!

7. ____   What is she drinking? I have to call the poison control center!

B. Look and write the letters A–G.

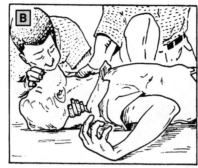

1. __E__ They're calling the emergency number. They need the police right away.

2. _____ She's giving artificial respiration.

3. _____ She's pressing on her skin with a clean cloth. Is she stopping the blood?

4. _____ He's putting a cold bandage on the burn.

5. _____ The paramedics are giving CPR (cardiopulmonary resuscitation). They're very careful.

6. _____ She may vomit.

7. _____ She's pressing on the place under his stomach.

PART TWO /LISTENING

● Emergencies and First Aid

 A. **Listen and write the numbers *1–4*.**

 B. **Listen and number the instructions *1–3*.**

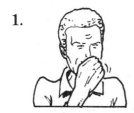      

1.   2.   3.

a. ____ He can't breathe, so put your arms around him.

____ First, is he coughing?

____ Press on the place under his stomach. Be careful.

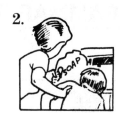

b. ____ Follow these instructions. First, give the child milk or water.

____ After that, drive him to the hospital.

____ Don't forget the soap bottle. Take it with you.

c. ____ Second, you put a clean cloth in cold water.

____ Then put it on the burn.

____ You put his arm in cold water.

d. ____ You can use a bandage later.

____ Put her hand up.

____ Get a clean cloth. Press on the skin with the cloth. She can sit or lie down.

PART THREE / GRAMMAR IN CONVERSATION

- The Present Continuous
- Emergency Help

	1		**you, 2+**	
yes	I'm Someone is He's She's	getting help.	We're Some people are They're	getting help.
no	I'm He's She's	not bleeding.	We're You're They're	not bleeding.

I'm	=	I am		
he's	=	he is	he isn't = he's not	
she's	=	she is	she isn't = she's not	
we're	=	we are	we aren't = we're not	
you're	=	you are	you aren't = you're not	
they're	=	they are	they aren't = they're not	

 A. **Listen and talk.**

1. **a:** Please **help us**!   call for help

   b: What's **wrong**?   the matter

   a: **This man** is   Someone
   having a heart attack.   choking
   And **he isn't** breathing.   she's not

2. **a:** Operator.

   b: Operator, **we need help**!   this is an emergency
   Please get us   We need
   an ambulance!   the paramedics!

3. **a:** This is the **emergency number**.
　　Tell us the address of the **emergency**.

  fire
  department
  What's
  emergency?

 b: It's 340 **Texas Place-between Main Street and Central**.
　　Apartment sixteen- on the **first** floor.

  Oak Drive
  north of Grand
  Avenue
  Number 303
  third

B. Have conversations.

EXAMPLE:
 a: Emergency.
 b: We need help right away. Someone is having a heart attack!
 a: The address, please?
 b: It's . . . .

1.

having a heart attack

2.

drowning

3.

bleeding badly

4.

choking

5.

not breathing

*6.

(an emergency)

	1		you, 2+	
Is	anyone / someone	helping?	Are	you / they	helping?
What is	the man / he	doing?	What are	you / the men	doing?
Where is	the girl / she	going?	When are	you / they	going?
How is it	going?		Why are	you / we	doing that?

 C. **Listen and talk.**

a: **Is someone** helping the **woman**?	Are you man
b: **My friend is** trying.	We're
a: What's **he** doing?	are you
b: **He's giving artificial respiration.**	I'm using a bandage.
a: Why **is he** doing that?	are you
b: Because **she's not breathing**.	he's bleeding

D. Have conversations.

EXAMPLE: **1. a:** Is someone helping the boy?
b: My wife is trying.
a: What's she doing?
b: She's pressing on the place under his stomach.
a: Why's she doing that?
b: Because he's choking.

1. she

pressing on the place under
   his stomach
he's choking

2. he

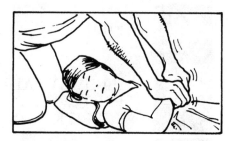

giving artificial respiration
she's not breathing

3. they

doing C.P.R.
there's no heartbeat

4. you / I

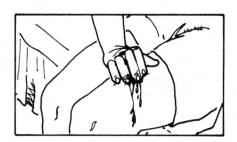

pressing on my skin
I have to stop the blood

5. we

putting on a cold, wet bandage
it's a bad burn

*6. you / I

(an emergency)

PART FOUR / READING AND WRITING

● Emergency Numbers, Instructions, and Signs

 A. **Read and write these telephone numbers.**

Here are examples of important telephone numbers. You can find the numbers for your city in your local telephone book.

EMERGENCY CALLS ONLY

 FIRE

 HIGHWAY PATROL
POLICE
SHERIFF

9-1-1

 PARAMEDICS

Poison Control Center 555-5151

OTHER CALLS

Springvale, City of
Fire Department 555-5000

Hospital 555-6109

Police Department 555-7311

1. __911__ There's a fire in your house. It's an emergency.

2. _____ Someone is trying to break into your apartment.

3. _____ You see a car accident. Some people are hurt.

4. _____ You want to talk to a sick friend. He's in the hospital.

5. _____ You want some information about the police department.

6. _____ Someone is having a heart attack.

7. _____ Your child has a bottle of poison in his hand and poison in his mouth.

_____ ## B. **Look in your local telephone book. Write the phone numbers for your city.**

EMERGENCY CALLS ONLY

FIRE .... _____

POLICE .... _____

PARAMEDICS .... _____

_____ , City of

Fire Department .... _____

Hospital .... _____

Poison Control Center .... _____

Police Department .... _____

C. Read and check (✓) the true sentences.

THE CALL FOR HELP

1. Someone needs emergency help but is breathing. What do you do?

   —Call an emergency number right away.

2. Someone isn't breathing. What do you do?

   —Help first and call later. Or send another person to the telephone.

3. How do you make an emergency phone call?

   —Call the telephone number. Wait for an answer.

   —Give your phone number.

   —Give the address of the emergency.

   —Tell about the emergency.

   —Say and spell your name.

   —Don't hang up. Wait for questions or information.

---

1. ____ Someone needs help but is breathing. Call an emergency number right away.

2. ____ A person isn't breathing. Go to a telephone right away.

3. ____ In an emergency, try to help. Send another person to the telephone.

4. ____ In an emergency phone call, tell the person's name and weight first.

5. ____ In an emergency call, tell your phone number and the place or address of the emergency first.

6. ____ Then tell about the problem or emergency.

7. ____ In an emergency, tell the problem and then hang up the phone right away.

D. Look and write the letters *A–H.*

1. __C__ Don't swim here. It can be dangerous.

2. ____ You can park here only in an emergency.

3. ____ Be careful with this. Don't give it to your children.

4. ____ You can't drive in here. You have to go around.

5. ____ This truck has dangerous things in it.

6. ____ A wet road can be dangerous.

7. ____ You can call for emergency help here.

8. ____ Be careful. People are working on the road.

CHAPTER

9

Work

COMPETENCIES:
Knowing how to look for work
Describing past work, job skills, and education
Understanding educational requirements
Understanding "help wanted" ads
Reading and filling out applications for employment

GRAMMAR FOCUS:
The simple past tense

I worked in a hospital and took care of patients.

PART ONE / VOCABULARY

● Jobs and Work

A. Look and write the letters *A–F*.

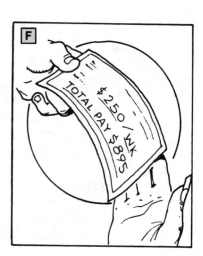

1. _E_ This job isn't permanent. And it's not full-time.

2. ____ He's telling about his job skills and experience at this job interview.

3. ____ She's studying the "Help Wanted" ads.

4. ____ They're filling out applications for employment.

5. ____ They're visiting an employment agency.

6. ____ I'm getting my paycheck.

B. Look and write the letters *A–H*.

"What about experience? What did you do in your last job?"

A — a teacher's aide	B — a secretary
C — a deliveryperson	D — a hospital worker	E — a waitress
F — a parking attendant	G — a salesclerk	H — a student

1. __D__ He took care of patients. He worked with machines.

2. ____ I worked with children in a grade school. I read to them and helped them with their schoolwork.

3. ____ She didn't cook. But she waited on people in a restaurant.

4. ____ He typed and answered the phone. He took messages.

5. ____ He drove a truck and delivered food.

6. ____ I have a high school diploma and a certificate from a business school. I got good grades. But I don't have a college degree.

7. ____ She helped customers in a store. She used a computer.

8. ____ I parked cars. It wasn't very interesting.

PART TWO / LISTENING

- Job Ads and Interviews (Skills, Education, and Experience)

 A. **Listen and write the numbers 1–4.**

B.   **Listen and follow the instructions.**

1. Circle the job ad.

Cook Needed 9 months a year Sept.-June 9 a.m.-2 p.m. **The Corner School**	**Temporary Teacher's Aide** part-time Mon. Wed. Fri. 9 a.m.-1 p.m. **The Corner School**	**Secretary Permanent Position** Tues. and Thurs. only. 8 a.m.-4 p.m. **The Corner School**	**Office Clerk** full-time Mon.-Fri. 9 a.m.-5 p.m. **The Corner School**

2. Check (✓) Ms. Wilson's four job skills.

☐ can type   ☐ does math well

☐ reads and writes English well   ☐ drives a truck

☐ knows Spanish   ☐ can deliver machines

☐ can use computers   ☐ can answer the phone and take messages

3. Circle two pictures.

1972   1978   1982   1986

HIGH SCHOOL DIPLOMA   CALIFORNIA COLLEGE OF BUSINESS DEGREE   NIGHT SCHOOL CLASSES ENGLISH/MATH   TEACHING CERTIFICATE

4. Check (✓) Ms. Wilson's experience.

☐ cleaned houses and offices   ☐ sold English and math books

☐ parked cars   ☐ is a housewife

☐ typed on a computer   ☐ helps children with schoolwork

☐ waited on customers   ☐ takes care of patients in a hospital

PART THREE / GRAMMAR IN CONVERSATION

- The Simple Past - Jobs Ads and Interviews

 A. **Listen and talk.**

a: <u>A-1 Computers.</u>   XYZ Company.

b: <u>Good afternoon.</u>   Hello.
<u>Can I have information</u>   I'm calling
about your ad
for a **salesclerk?**   cashier.

a: <u>Of course.</u> Well,   Sure.
it's a **full-time** job.   temporary
You work **five days** a week—   twenty hours
<u>from 9:00 a.m.</u>   in the
<u>to 5:00 p.m.</u>   afternoon.
And **the pay is**   you get
$1200 a month. $220 a week

b: <u>All right.</u>   Fine.
<u>When can I come in for</u>   When can I have
an interview?

*B. **Have conversations.**

1.

> **Office Clerk Wanted**
> full-time
> 6 days/week   8:00-4:30
> $1400/month
> **Fifth Street School**
> 4500 Fifth St.

2.

> **Cook Needed**
> part-time
> FRI., SAT., SUN.
> 5:00-10:30 p.m.
> $260/week
> **Pete's Pizza**

3.

> **Truck Driver**
> permanent position
> Monday-Friday
> 40-50 hours/week
> $12/hour
> **Dan's Delivery Company**

4.

> **Teacher's Aide**
> temporary position
> Mon., Wed., Fri.
> 9:00 a.m.-1:00 p.m.
> $5/hr.
> **The Corner School**

C. **Listen and talk.**

a: Hello. **I'm** Pat Miller.   My name is

b: **I'm glad** to meet you,   Nice
   Mr. Miller.   Ms.

   Let's start with your job skills.   Tell me about
   Can you **type**?   drive a truck

a: **No, I can't.**   Yes, I can.
   And I **can't use a computer**.   can drive a bus
   But I can learn.   I can deliver things.

b: What **can you do**?   are your other skills

a: I can **do math well**.   park cars
   And I speak **three languages**.   Spanish and Chinese

D. **Have conversations.**

EXAMPLE: **1. a:** Can you cook?
           b: Yes, I can. I cook well. And I can clean houses.

1.    2.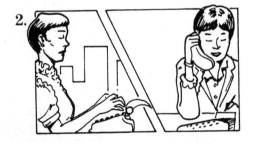

3.    *4.

your job skills

	now		in the past
I	'm a salesclerk. work in an office. study business. drive a truck. read books. sell clothing.	I	was a salesclerk. worked in an office. studied business. drove a truck. read books. sold clothing.

work	/ worked	be	/ was, were
study	/ studied	take	/ took
wait	/ waited	drive	/ drove
talk	/ talked	sell	/ sold
answer	/ answered	go	/ went
deliver	/ delivered	get	/ got

E. Listen and talk.

1. **a:** Tell me about your **first job**.

   b: From 1972 to 1975
   I was **a parking attendant**
   for **a restaurant**.
   I **parked cars**
   and **talked to people**.

   job experience

   In my first job
   an office clerk
   an insurance company
   answered the telephone
   took messages

2. **a: What about your next position?**

   b: I worked in a **pizza place**.
   I **drove a truck**
   and **delivered food**.

   And after that?

   men's shop
   waited on customers
   sold clothing

3. **a: What do you do** now?

   b: I'm a **nurse's** aide.
   I **take patients' temperatures**.
   And I **take care of** them.

   What's your job

   teacher's
   teach children math
   read to

F. Have conversations.

EXAMPLE:
1. a: Tell me about your experience.
   b: Well in my first job I was a parking attendant. I worked for a restaurant. I parked cars and took care of them.

1.

WORK EXPERIENCE			
Date	**Position**	**Employer**	**Work**
from 1979 to 1980	a parking attendant	a restaurant	parked cars took care of them
from 1980 to 1983	a nurse's aide	a hospital	took temperatures checked information
from 1985 to 1987	an office clerk	a school	typed answered the phone
from 1987 to now	a computer operator	an insurance company	do math use computers

*2.

WORK EXPERIENCE			
Date	**Position**	**Employer**	**Work**
from to	(your first job)		
from to	(your next job)		
from to	(your job now)		

Were	you	a student?			finish high school?
Was	your teacher	good?	Did you		take a typing class?
Were	your grades	O.K.?			get a degree?

Yes,	I	was.	Yes,		did.
No,	he / she	wasn't.	No,	I	didn't.

Yes,	they	were.
No,		weren't.

Who	was	your boss?	Where		go to college?
How	were	your grades?	When	did you	leave school?

 G.   **Listen and talk.**

1. a: Did you **finish high school**?   get a high school diploma

　 b: **Yes, I did.**   No, I didn't.

　 a: When did you **get your diploma**?   leave school

　 b: **Five years ago.**   Last year.

　 a: Were **you a good student**?   your grades good

　 b: **Yes, I was.**   No, they weren't.

2. a: Did you **go to college**?   take other classes

　 b: **No, I didn't.**   Yes, I did.

　 a: **But I went to a language school.**   I took typing.
      And I **got a certificate**.   studied business

H. Have conversations.

EXAMPLE: **1. a:** When did you finish grade school?
          b: In 1971.
          a: Did you get a high school diploma?
          a: Yes, I did. I went to high school from 1971 to 1975. I studied English and math.

1.

EDUCATION			
	Dates	Classes	Degree?
GRADE SCHOOL	from 1963 to 1971		
HIGH SCHOOL	from 1971 to 1975	English, math	diploma
BUSINESS SCHOOL	from 1975 to 1977	typing, computers	certificate
NIGHT SCHOOL	from 1987 to now	cooking	no
COLLEGE	from to		

*2.

EDUCATION			
	Dates	Classes	Degree?
GRADE SCHOOL	from to		
HIGH SCHOOL	from to		
BUSINESS SCHOOL	from to		
NIGHT SCHOOL	from to		
COLLEGE	from to		

PART FOUR / READING AND WRITING

- Applications for Employment

Name	Vargas Mario	Social Security Number	495-66-7042
	last first		

Address 1007 Prince St.   Telephone (212) 555-8010

Date Oct. 28   City and State Peoria IL

Education

Delmar H.S.	Chicago, Illinois		1983-86	Math
High School	Location		Dates	Main Subjects

Work Experience (Put present or last job first.)

Date (Month and Year)	Name and Location of Employer	Salary	Position	Reason for Leaving
From 1/88 To now	Brentwood Cinema Peoria	$6/ hour	ticket taker	—
From 7/86 To 10/87	Uncle Joe's Cafe Chicago	$5/ hour	busboy	moved

A. Read and answer the questions.

1. In what month did Mario apply for a job? _____

2. What's Mario's social security number? _____

3. What job does he have now? _____

4. How much is he making now? _____

5. Did Mario go to high school? _____ Did he finish high school? _____

   Did he get a degree from computer school? _____

6. When was Mario a busboy? _____ Did he make $5 an hour? _____

   Why did he leave that job? _____

*B. Write the information about you.

Name _____   Social Security Number _____
　　　　　last　　　　first

Address _____   Telephone _____

Date _____   City and State _____

Education

Grammar School	Location		Dates	
High School	Location		Dates	Main Subjects
Trade / Vocational School	Location		Dates	Main Subjects

Do not write below this line.

Work Experience (Put present or last job first.)

	Date (Month and Year)	Name and Location of Employer	Salary	Position	Reason for Leaving
From	_____	_____	_____	_____	_____
To	_____	_____	_____	_____	_____
From	_____	_____	_____	_____	_____
To	_____	_____	_____	_____	_____

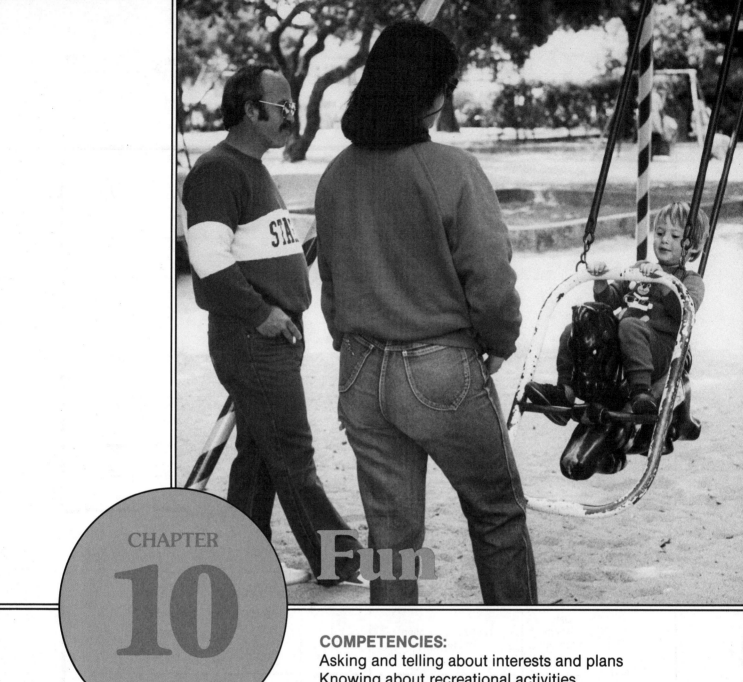

CHAPTER
10

Fun

COMPETENCIES:
Asking and telling about interests and plans
Knowing about recreational activities
Understanding party invitations
Understanding T.V. and radio schedules
Reading recreation programs and information

GRAMMAR FOCUS:
The future (*going to*)

What are you going to do today?

PART ONE / VOCABULARY

● Sports and Recreational Activities

A. Look and write the letters *A–H*.

1. __G__ First I'm going to go swimming at the high school pool.

2. _____ Then we're going to ride our bikes in the park.

3. _____ This afternoon there's going to be a football game.

4. _____ Tonight we're going to watch a movie on Channel 5. We aren't going to listen to the radio.

5. _____ Let's go shopping tomorrow.

6. _____ I'm interested in sports—tennis and soccer.

7. _____ We can learn to play cards at the city's recreation program.

8. _____ Next weekend there's going to be a party with guitar music and dancing.

PART TWO / LISTENING

● Plans ● Party Invitations ● T.V. Programs ● Recreational Classes

 A.   **Listen and write the numbers *1–4*.**

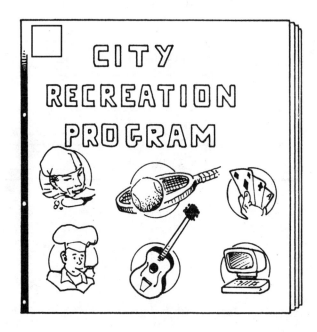

B.   **Listen and follow the instructions.**

1. Number the pictures 1–4.

2. Circle the words.

IT'S A PARTY!

Where? At	school. / the boss's house.
When? On	Friday, June 12. / Saturday, July 20.

What?	Music / Games	and	movies. / dancing.
Why?	It's the	first / last	day of class.

3. Write the words.

movie	swimming	dancing	soccer	football

T.V. Today			T.V. Today		
CHANNEL	TIME		CHANNEL	TIME	
4	10:00	_____ game	7	12:00	_____
8	10:30	_____ game	8	12:30	_____
11	11:30	_____			

4. Check (✓) four classes.

☐ Tennis, Level 1   ☐ Swimming   ☐ Guitar   ☐ Card Games

☐ Tennis, Level 2   ☐ Dancing for Exercise   ☐ Cooking   ☐ Home Computers

PART THREE / GRAMMAR IN CONVERSATION

● The Future (*going to*) ● Interests and Plans

 A. Listen and talk.

a: **Why don't you tell me** about your **interests?**   I want to know interests.

b: **What do you want to know?**   All right.

a: Well, do you like **sports**?   movies

b: **Yes, I do.**   Not really.

a: Are you interested in **games**?   languages

b: **Yes, I am.**   No, I'm not.

a: **What about** other interests?   Do you have

b: I like to **play the guitar**.   go shopping

*B. Have conversations with three classmates. Check the boxes and write information.

EXAMPLE: a: Hello, Felicia. I want to know about your interests.
b: Sure. Well, I'm interested in sports.
a: Uh-huh. And do you like music?

NAME	SPORTS?	MUSIC?	MOVIES?	GAMES?	OTHER

	1			you, 2+	
I'm		study.	We're		study.
My friend is	going to	cook.	You're	going to	cook.
He's / She's		go out.	They're		go out.

C. Listen and talk.

a: **I'm** going to
   go to the park
   this afternoon.
   Do you want to go
   with **me**?

   A friend is
   go shopping
   tomorrow
   Let's
   him

b: **I want to**,
   but I **don't have time**.
   I have to **visit the doctor**.
   And then **I'm** going to
   watch T.V.

   Thanks
   can't
   work
   we're
   clean the house

D. Make sentences.

EXAMPLE: 1. I'm going to go to the doctor tomorrow morning.

1. I / tomorrow morning

2. We / this evening

3. she / tonight

4. he / next Monday

5. they / this weekend

*6. I

(your plans)

1				you, 2+	
Is	your friend he she	going to call?	Are	you we they	going to call?

What Where When How Why	am I are we are you is he is she	going to	do? go? leave? get there? do that?	

E. Listen and talk.

1. **a:** What are **you** going to
do **tonight**?

   your friends
next weekend

   b: **I'm** going to
watch T.V.

   They're
have a party

2. **a:** Why are **you** going to
watch T.V.?

   they
give a party

   b: Because **there's a good
movie on Channel 9.**

   they want to
meet people

3. **a:** Where are **you** going to
go tomorrow?

   they
cook the food

   b: **To a soccer game.**

   At their place.

4. **a:** When is the **game** going
to **start**?

   party
be

   b: **At 11:00 in the morning.**

   Saturday night.

5. **a:** How are **you** going
to get there?

   we

   b: **Let's take the bus.**

   We can walk.

*F.   Ask questions and answer them.

EXAMPLES: a: What are you going to do tomorrow?
b: I'm going to take a long ride in a bus.
a: Really? Why are you going to do that?
b: Because I want to see the city.

1. What | are / is | you / we / your family | going to do | tonight? / tomorrow? / this weekend?

2. Why are | you / we / they | going to do that?

3. Where are | you / we / they | going to go?

4. When are | you / we | going to | leave? / come home?

5. How are | you / we | going to | get there? / get home?

6. What | is / are | your _____ / your _____s | going to do?

PART FOUR / READING AND WRITING

● Recreation Programs and Information

 A. **Read and answer the questions on page 142.**

City Recreation Program

The city recreation program for adults is going to begin next September.

Recreational Swimming $2.00
                                                          every time

City High School Pool - 1334 4th St.
Mon.-Thurs. 7:00-9:30 p.m.   Fri. 6:00-7:30 p.m.

The water temperature is 80°. The pool is open from Sept. 16 to Dec. 20. No application is necessary. Just come!

Dance for Exercise $2.50
                                                          every time

Street Park Gymnasium
Tuesday 6:00-7:00 p.m. or 7:00-8:00 p.m.   Thursday 6:30-8:00 p.m.

Exercise to the music and feel good. No application is necessary.

Card Games $32.00

City College Cafeteria
Monday 7:30-10:00 p.m.   9/15-10/27

Learn to play cards well and meet new people. No experience needed.

Small Computers $18.00

Room 200, City High School
6 meetings 9/17 - 10/28   Wed. 8:00-10:00 p.m. or Sat. 9:30-11:30 a.m.

Learn about your home computer and try new programs.

Guitar Level 1 $28.00

Oak Street Park Recreation Room
Saturday 10:00 a.m. to 2:00 p.m.   10/4-12/20

Learn to play. Have fun with music.

Cooking for Men and Boys $32.00

High School Cooking Room
Thurs. 7:00-9:30 p.m.   9/18-12/4

Learn to cook good food. We're going to eat, too!

1. In what class are people going to exercise? _____

   play games? _____   play music? _____

2. Where are people going to go swimming? _____

   cook and eat? _____   learn about computers? _____

3. How many times can they go swimming in a week? _____

   take a guitar class? _____

4. What day of the week does the cooking class meet? _____

   the guitar class? _____

5. What time does the dance class begin on Tuesdays? _____

   on Thursdays? _____

6. What time is the card game class going to end? _____

   the computer class on Saturdays? _____

7. What's the first date of the guitar class? _____

   the last date of the cooking class? _____

8. In what months can people swim at the high school? _____

   learn card games? _____

9. How much is one dance class going to cost? _____

   the six-week computer class? _____

_____ **B.** **Fill out the application form for you.**

CITY RECREATIONAL PROGRAM FOR ADULTS		
Name _____ Driver's License Number _____		
1. Class _____ Place _____		
Dates _____ Time _____ Price _____		
2. Class _____ Place _____		
Dates _____ Time _____ Price _____		

C. Look and write the letters A–F.

A

It's a Party!

Time _____

Day _____

Date _____

Place _____

_____

Come and have fun!!

TWO DINNERS FOR THE PRICE OF ONE

C

Buy one dinner at the regular price
and get the 2nd FREE!

Uncle John's Fine Food
3201 Eastlake Blvd.

B   **Nov. 1-7**

T.V. Programs

D

ADMIT 1

Sun., 2/14   **8:15**
Doors open at 7:30

The Music Hall
135 N. Note Ave.

E

You're going to like this movie!

The Long, Hot Year

**Now playing at
the CINEMAR Theaters**

F   Radio   AM   KLUV   780   KGUD   1150   KKOK   1460
                FM   KFUN   98.3   KJOY   103.1   KROK   90.6

1. _C_ You can use this at a restaurant. Two people can eat dinner, but they pay for only one.

2. ____ Use this ticket in February. You're going to hear some music.

3. ____ This book tells the programs on television for a week.

4. ____ This information about a movie is from a newspaper.

5. ____ A class is going to have a party at school.

6. ____ This list tells the names of stations and their numbers on the radio.